Cla

An Ayrshireman, Dane Love lives in the countryside near Cumnock. He works as a schoolteacher at Irvine Royal Academy, but enjoys travelling with his wife around Scotland doing research. He is interested in all aspects of Scottish history, and has written histories of the Ayrshire towns and villages of Ayr, Cumnock and Auchinleck. With an interest in genealogy, he has traced his ancestry back to one Robin Love, his six-times great grandfather, who fought with Bonnie Prince Charlie at the battles of Prestonpans and Culloden. His books include *Scottish Kirkyards, Scottish Ghosts* and *The Auld Inns of Scotland* all published by Robert Hale.

By the same author

Scottish Kirkyards
Scottish Ghosts
The Auld Inns of Scotland

Tales
of the
Clan Chiefs

DANE LOVE

ROBERT HALE · LONDON

© *Dane Love 1999*
First published in Great Britain 1999

ISBN 0 7090 6273 7

Robert Hale Limited
Clerkenwell House
Clerkenwell Green
London EC1R 0HT

2 4 6 8 10 9 7 5 3 1

Typeset in North Wales by
Derek Doyle & Associates, Mold, Flintshire.
Printed in Great Britain by
St Edmundsbury Press Limited, Bury St Edmunds
and bound by
WBC Book Manufacturers Limited, Bridgend

Contents

Introduction

Scotland is famous for its clans. The word derives from the Gaelic *clann*, which means literally 'children, family or offspring'. The tradition of belonging to a family group for greater protection survived in Scotland long after it had died out in other western countries, and many people throughout the world today enjoy the right to claim membership of particular Scottish clans, united in a common ancestry.

The Scottish and British parliaments passed acts which recognised the existence of these clans. One of these, an Act of Parliament passed by James VI in 1587, listed 'The roll of the clannis that hes capitanes, cheiffis and chiftanes quhome on thay depend oftymes aganis the willis of thair landislordis'. This roll noted 34 Highland clans.

In a number of cases the government issued commissions which were better known as 'Letters of Fire and Sword' to deal with unruly clans or clansmen. Invoked when the normal criminal justice system was too weak to deal with the law-breakers, these allowed neighbouring chiefs or landlords the use of unrestricted force to deal with such offenders. In a time of constant feud, these letters of fire and sword were often abused by clan chiefs to allow them to continue their feuds with the backing of the government.

The clans of Scotland are often thought to have existed in the Highlands only, but an Act of the Scots Parliament of 1552 refers to 'the clannys of Liddisdale and Eskdaill'. There were indeed clans throughout the Border countryside and in south-west Scotland, but they were pacified and subjected to national laws a century or two before those of the Highlands. This book will tell tales of Highland clan chiefs only.

The vast majority of the tales are true, for documentary evidence of the stories survives in old charters, accounts and records. However, the tales were also handed down by word of mouth, and the original seanchaidh or Highland storytellers elaborated them as and when required, so that some of them may be a bit suspect. The introduction of superhuman feats and black magic can probably be attributed to these tellers of tales. Who is to question them, though? The account of the witches and the Chief of the Munros is well documented in contemporary court records – although the great green toad which accompanied the Chief of the Clanranald MacDonalds is harder to explain!

Virtually every clan chief in the past had some tale told about him – whether of daring feats of cattle rustling, feuds with other clans, raids on the lowlands or attacking passing ships. In a book such as this only a few can be recounted, and in general I have stuck to those associated with a single chief – some of which are in danger of being forgotten, even by members of the clans concerned.

I hope that this book may rekindle an interest in searching out information on the history of the clans. A number of detailed histories of some of the larger clans have been written in the past, and a few of the smaller clans are now producing accounts of their heritage. Readers who belong to a specific clan may find much of interest if they search out some of these (often long out of print) volumes. Alternatively, they may wish to support the growing number of clan societies throughout the world, which produce newsletters and other literature on the history of their ancestors. A few clan societies have even established their own museums; the first of these was the Clan MacPherson Museum at Newtonmore; and one of the most ambitious is the restoration of Castle Menzies by the Menzies Clan Society. A number of clan associations have even repurchased some of the ancestral lands, where these have been sold or lost by their chiefs. The greatest example is the Clan Donald Lands Trust, which purchased 20,000 acres of Skye, including the ruins of Armadale Castle. A visitor centre welcomes sons of Donald from all corners of the globe, and a genealogical centre helps them to find their roots.

DANE LOVE
Auchinleck, 1998

Illustrations

Tales
of the
Clan Chiefs

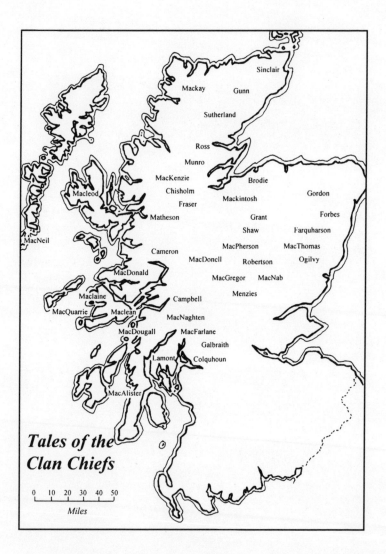

Sinclair

Mackay   Gunn

Sutherland

Ross
Munro

MacKenzie   Brodie
Chisholm   Gordon
          Mackintosh
Fraser
                              Forbes
Matheson   Grant
              Shaw   Farquharson

MacNeil   MacPherson   MacThomas
          Cameron
                  MacDoncll   Robertson   Ogilvy
          MacDonald
                  MacGregor   MacNab

Maclaine   Campbell
                              Menzies
MacQuarrie   Maclean
          MacDougall   MacNaghten

                  MacFarlane
                  Galbraith
          Lamont   Colquhoun

MacAlister

Tales of the Clan Chiefs

0   10   20   30   40   50

Miles

I   Brodie of that Ilk
The Rebel Chief

Brodie Castle, a very fine building which stands seven miles east of
Nairn, was passed to the National Trust for Scotland in 1980 by
Ninian Brodie of Brodie, 25th Chief. Before that it had been the seat
of the clan chiefs ever since it was built. The oldest part of the castle,
which has been extended on a number of occasions, dates from the
second half of the sixteenth century, but the Brodies are reckoned to
have owned these lands from before 1311, when Michael Brodie of
that Ilk was given a charter of confirmation by Robert the Bruce.
However, the clan's ancient charters were lost when Brodie Castle
was burned in 1646 by Lord Lewis Gordon, afterwards the third
Marquis of Huntly.

Our tale concerns Alexander Brodie of that Ilk, who succeeded as
12th Chief sometime around 1550, on the death of his father, also
Alexander. Alexander the younger married twice, his first wife
giving him a son and heir, David (1553–1626), and his second wife a
further five sons and five daughters.

Alexander took part in a raid on the lands of the Cummings of
Altyre in the mid-sixteenth century. The Cummings were a powerful clan in the district – too powerful according to many – and
Alexander Brodie was one of 127 clansmen who set an ambush on a
roadway outside Forres. Amongst others present was John Hay, son
of the laird of Castle of Park. The party hid themselves amongst the
trees and bushes beside the roadway and waited silently. As
Alexander Cumming, chief of that clan, passed by, Brodie's men
rushed out waving their claymores and dirks and attacked Cumming
and his retainers. A number of the Cummings were wounded in the
affray, and all had to flee to safety. No lives seem to have been lost,
though one of Cumming's servants was wounded. The Brodies then

Brodie Castle

headed for Altyre, the Cumming chief's castle, and destroyed some of his property there.

The Cumming chief complained to the authorities about the attack (which a contemporary record described as 'umbesetting'), and a warrant was issued for Alexander Brodie's arrest. The countryside was searched for him, but he refused to stand trial for his part in the raid. As a result, in November 1550, he and the other men involved in the attack were denounced as rebels, or 'put to the horn' in the old parlance. No record survives of Alexander being punished for his actions.

He later joined the Roman Catholic George Gordon, fourth Earl of Huntly, in his opposition to Mary Queen of Scots when she came north to Aberdeenshire and Moray in 1562. Lord James Stewart of Darnaway Castle was created Earl of Moray by the Queen, an honour that Huntly had assumed would be his. As a result, Huntly was joined by one thousand men, including Alexander Brodie, and marched towards Aberdeen. The new Earl of Moray advanced from Aberdeen with 2,000 men, and both forces met at the Battle of Corrichie on 28 October 1562. In the battle, which took place on the slopes of the Hill o' Fare in Deeside, Moray was the victor.

As a consequence of his part in the battle Brodie's estates were forfeited, but in 1566 Mary Queen of Scots pardoned Brodie, and his estates were returned to him. The old castle of Brodie seems to have suffered in the intervening years, and so the chief decided to do some rebuilding. This took the form of a Z-plan tower-house, the entrance to which was probably on the first floor, reached by a removable ladder; the ground floor contained the vaulted kitchens (converted into the present entrance hall) and a guard chamber. The present south-west tower, distinguished by its spiral stair, was also Alexander's work, and is dated 1567 on the gable. The older castle seems to have been demolished at the time.

Alexander Brodie seems to have settled down after he built his new castle, for history records no further major misdemeanours against his name. He may have expended most of his energies on improving his estate. He died in 1583 and was succeeded by his eldest son, David Brodie of that Ilk.

2   Cameron of Lochiel
The Lochan of the Sword

At the head of Rannoch is a fairly small loch which is marked on the map as Lochan a' Chlaidheimh, or 'loch of the sword' in English. Its location at the junction of the old counties of Argyll, Perth and Inverness tends to indicate that it lay at the junction of three estates and was at one time an important boundary marker. Indeed, it was the site of a notable incident between the Camerons and Murrays.

Ewen MacAllan Cameron, the 13th Chief of the Camerons, was born some time in the late fifteenth century and succeeded his father, Allan Cameron, around 1480. His lands extended eastward to Rannoch, but the actual boundary was disputed. Both he and the Earl of Atholl, who owned Rannoch at that time, claimed the important grazing lands of Black Water and Beinn a' Bhreac. Arguments raged over the line of the boundary, for there were no obvious natural features to follow. It was eventually decided that both Cameron and the Earl of Atholl should meet on the lands and settle the matter once and for all. Only two men were to accompany each chief – his personal piper and one other.

Ewen Cameron took two of his men and began his journey through the mighty mountains of Lochaber towards the lochan. On their journey they came across an old woman known as Gormshuil, or 'blue eye', who lived at a cottage called Moy, four miles south-west of Achnacarry (the present seat of the Cameron chiefs) and three miles north-east of Torcastle, their seat in the fifteenth century. She had a reputation as a witch or seer, and many times in the past she had warned the chiefs of dangers – enabling them to change their plans and prevent major disaster.

'Hail, Cameron of Lochiel, from your kinswoman, Gormshuil of

Moy. Where are you going with just two attendants?' asked the old woman.

'I'm heading for the Lochan a' Chlaidheimh, to settle a boundary dispute with Murray of Atholl,' Cameron replied. 'You know that it has long been a source of trouble between the clans, and I hope to come to a final settlement in a friendly manner this day.'

'Go back, Lochiel, go back!' the witch replied. 'There is a trap being prepared for you by the laird of Atholl. Gather together three score and five of the best fighting men at your disposal. Should their assistance be required then they will be near at hand. If they are not required, then so much the better.'

Ewen Cameron returned to his castle and summoned some men. Again he set off for the lochan, this time with a crack fighting force at his disposal. They reached Leanachan by nightfall, and rested there. Ewen Cameron gathered his men around him and explained what their plan was to be. He would wear a large cloak lined in scarlet, and would go alone to talk to Murray, and his men were to remain a short distance behind, concealed on the hillside. Should the negotiations go smoothly, he would keep his cloak on, the grey side outermost. However, if he ran into difficulties, and things began to look decidedly violent, he would pull off his cloak and turn it inside out, so that the red lining would be visible for hundreds of yards across the moor.

The next morning Cameron led his men towards the lochan. When they had concealed themselves on the slopes of Meall Liath na Doire, Cameron walked down to the loch, where he met Murray. They discussed the problem for some time, each suggesting where the boundary line should run, but neither would give in to the other. When things began to get more heated, Murray held up his arm, and suddenly a number of men appeared from the heather and made their way towards the two chiefs.

'Who are these men, Lord Atholl?' Ewen inquired.

'These are just some Atholl wethers [rams], which have come to graze the meadows alongside the Black Water, which belong to me,' Murray replied.

Seeing that Murray was about to use foul means to win the dispute, Cameron whipped off his cloak, and turned it inside out. At the signal, 65 men jumped up from the hillside behind him, and made their way down to join their chief.

'Who are these?' Murray inquired.

'These are just some Lochaber dogs, hungry for a taste of some

Atholl mutton,' replied Cameron. 'Give up your claim to the lands, for I will be unable to hold them back for very long.'

Realising that there were more Cameron men than Atholl men, Murray acquiesced and gave up his claim to the lands. As a sign that the dispute was settled, he drew his sword from its sheath, kissed it, and threw it into the dark waters of the lochan. From that day to this, the loch has been known as the lochan of the sword – it marked the eastern boundary of the Cameron lands for over four centuries (until the lands hereabouts were sold by Cameron Lochiel in 1892). The rallying cry and war pibroch of the Camerons, 'Clanna nan con, thigibh a so, 's gheibh sibh feoil!' is reckoned to have originated at this time. It means, 'Children of the dogs, come here, and get flesh!'

There is an interesting 'confirmation' of this story. Around 1826 some men were fishing the loch from a small boat. Their lines became tangled in something on the bottom, and when they managed to pull them up an ancient and rusty broadsword came with them. The men took it to the minister at Kilmonivaig, near Spean Bridge, who was known to be a historian of some note. However, word reached some Cameron men, who felt that the sword should remain in the loch to mark the boundary of the lands. Twelve of them – four from Nether Lochaber, four from Locharkaig and four from Lochyside – went to the manse and asked the minister if he would give them the sword, so that they could return it. The minister passed it over, and the twelve men marched across the hills to Lochan a' Chlaidheimh where they ceremoniously threw it back into the waters.

Ewen MacAllan Cameron was a noted chief in his day and lived a long life, but one which was full of bloodshed and feud. In 1491 he took part in the 'Raid of Ross' and he was subsequently appointed Constable of the Wester Ross castle of Strome. In 1495 he received a charter from James IV confirming him in the lands of Lochiel. He remained in royal favour for a time thereafter, but in 1503 he became involved in the rising of Donald Dubh, who wished to reclaim the Lordship of the Isles, and was then denounced as a rebel. Shortly afterwards, in 1505, he is thought to have been responsible for the murder of Sir William Munro of Foulis, 12th Chief of that clan, at Achnashellach in Wester Ross. The reason for the murder is unclear, but it is said that Munro and the Mackays had joined forces to raid the area, which came under Cameron's jurisdiction as Constable of Strome.

The head of Ewen MacAllan Cameron on Elgin burgh gate

Ewen married twice. By his first wife, a daughter of MacDonald of Lochalsh, he had a son, Donald, who married Anne Grant, daughter of the chief of that clan. Later he married again, to Marjory, sister of the 13th Chief of Clan Mackintosh. When his son Donald predeceased him in 1537 Ewen's outlook on life changed. He became devoutly religious, and turned to peaceable pastimes. According to an old tradition, he consulted Gormshuil, the Witch of Moy, to find out how he could mitigate his sins. She told him to catch a black cat and take it to a wooden hut in the middle of a field, since known as Dail a' Chait, or 'field of the cat'. He was to pierce it with a spit and roast it over a fire. The cat screeched loudly in pain, attracting hundreds of cats from all over Lochaber. These had the miraculous ability to speak, and they asked him why he was torturing their cousin. Ewen asked what he would have to do to get forgiveness for his past sins. 'Build six churches and dedicate them to six different saints,' was the reply. Ewen then threw the roasted cat into the River Lochy, the pool of which has since been known as Poll a' Chait, and went on to build the old churches of Arisaig, Kilchoan, Cille Choirill, Kildonan, Kilkellan and Kilmallie. (Other accounts of the building of the six churches give a more religious attribution. It is said that Ewen Cameron set out on a pilgrimage to Rome, but fell ill on the way. He sent his priest to finish the journey and to ask the Pope how he could receive forgiveness for his sins. The priest returned with the order that he was to build the churches and dedicate them to six different saints.)

Although Ewen Cameron had become religious, he still found himself embroiled in the campaigns of the claimants to the Lordship of the Isles. He fought at the Battle of the Shirts, or Blar na Leine, in 1544, at which the Frasers were virtually wiped out (See Chapter 8). For this involvement and other crimes, he was arrested, tried in Elgin and found guilty. He was beheaded there in 1546, and his head was placed on a spike and displayed over the town gate. He was succeeded in the chiefship by his grandson, Ewen Beag, or little Ewen.

3   Campbell of Argyll
Abduction of an Heiress

The ancient castle of Cawdor stands in Strathnairn, south of Nairn. It has been a seat of the Campbell family since around 1500, now represented by Colin Campbell, seventh Earl of Cawdor. The castle is an extremely fine one, and visitors are welcomed to it throughout the summer months. Here one can see the ancient holly bush which is associated with the foundation of the castle in the fourteenth century.

According to the tale, William Calder of that Ilk, Thane of Cawdor, decided to build himself a new castle, but he was unsure where to build it. In a dream one night a vision appeared to him which told him how to decide the spot. He was to load up his donkey with his kist of gold coins and allow it to roam freely around his lands. Wherever the donkey lay down to rest at nightfall he was to build his castle, and the family would prosper thereafter. William did this, and as the sun set the donkey lay down to rest beneath the spreading branches of a holly tree.

William Calder (or Cawdor, as the name was pronounced) built his castle where the tree grew, but decided that he would preserve it. He therefore built around it, and the lowest vault of the original tower rises over it. Not unnaturally, the holly died from a lack of light and water starvation, but its trunk is still there, and when part of it was subjected to radiocarbon dating it was found to date from around 1372.

The Calders of that Ilk remained in possession of the castle until the death of John Calder, the eighth Chief in 1493. In 1492 John had married a local lass, Isabel or Elizabeth, daughter of Hugh Rose of Kilravock. Isabel turned out to be pregnant on her husband's death, and on 13 February 1493 she gave birth to twin daughters, Janet and

Muriel. Janet died within a year, and Muriel was left as the heiress to the estates. However, John Calder's brothers claimed that Muriel was an illegitimate child, and that her father denied responsibility for her on his deathbed – since she was a girl, they saw her as a threat to the Calder family succession to the lands.

In 1494 King James IV appointed Archibald, second Earl of Argyll, and Hugh Rose of Kilravock (her uncle) to be Muriel's tutors and guardians. However, at the time Hugh Rose was being tried on a charge of robbery (he had joined the chief of the Mackintoshes in raiding the lands belonging to Urquhart of Cromarty). Argyll felt that he had a greater claim to the girl's wardship, and in 1495 managed to persuade the king that he should bring up the girl. The Roses seem not to have accepted this, however, for Muriel remained with them. Nonetheless, Lord Argyll, the Chief of the Campbells, was an acquisitive man, and he saw in the situation an ideal opportunity to obtain an estate in which he could settle his third son, Sir John. In the autumn of 1499, therefore, when Muriel was six years old, he sent a kinsman, Campbell of Inverliever, with a force of sixty clansmen to kidnap the girl, who was staying at Kilravock Castle with her grandmother. The Inverliever Campbells attacked Kilravock and forced an entry into the ancient tower. As the Campbells made their way up the spiral stair, Muriel's nurse bit off the last joint of the girl's little finger, and her mother managed to heat a key in the fire, which she used to brand the girl on the hip. All this was to enable the Calder family to recognise the girl in future years if she grew up, and to check whether a false heiress was put in her place.

The girl was grabbed by the Campbells and they set off south with their prize. Word was quickly sent round the district, and her uncle, Hutcheon Calder, led a group of Calder and Rose horsemen in pursuit. At Daltulich, in Strathnairn, they spotted them in the distance, nursing a child in their arms, and managed to come upon them unseen. In the affray six Campbell men were killed, but, on inspection, the 'child' was discovered to be nothing but a sheaf of corn lifted from the fields and dressed in the child's clothes. The Campbells had been nursing it as a ruse; meanwhile a second group of Campbells, under Inverliever's son, had the girl, and they were able to return to Argyll with her.

Some tales say that one of the Campbell chieftains complained to the Earl of Argyll that the kidnap could be a waste of good clansmen's lives should the girl die. The Earl replied that the girl would never die so long as there was a red-haired lassie on the banks of Loch Awe (a reference to the fact that many Campbell women were flame-haired). The Calder heiress was kept by the Campbells, and brought up in comfort in their castles and as soon as she came of age (which at that time in Scotland was at twelve years old) was married to Argyll's third son, Sir John Campbell. On 17 February 1511 she passed the titles to her estates to her husband, confirming the transfer by appending her own personal seal. This document was signed at Castle Campbell, one of Lord Argyll's many towers, located above Dollar in Clackmannanshire. Lord Argyll died a couple of years later, fighting for James IV on the ill-fated field of Flodden in September 1513, and his eldest son, Colin, succeeded as the third Earl.

At first Sir John and Muriel Campbell lived on the lands of Muckairn in Argyll, where Sir John was the kirk's steward (he was later to acquire the lands by charter in 1532). Sir John's sister, Lady Elizabeth, married Lachlan Maclean of Duart, Chief of the Macleans, but her husband left her to drown on a rock, ever since known as the Lady's Rock. Sir John later came across Maclean in Edinburgh and ran a knife through his body, as recounted in Chapter 24. He was given remission for murder, but decided that it would be prudent to move north from Argyll, which was too near Duart, and so in 1524 he and his wife decided to return to Cawdor.

The welcome at Cawdor was not a warm one, for four of Muriel's uncles had taken over the castle and were claiming it for themselves. There was also ill-feeling because it was the tradition in Scotland that the husband of an heiress, if he was not an heir himself, should take the name of his wife, and thus allow the surname of her family to continue. Sir John had been expected to adopt the name Calder, but for some reason he was unwilling to do so, preferring instead to found a new family.

The Calder uncles attacked Cawdor, but were unsuccessful, and Roy Campbell and Donald MacAlistair (who had travelled north with Sir John and Muriel) managed to kill the heir-male of the Cawdors and his brother. This left the Calder family's position considerably weaker, and their claim to the castle was abandoned. The Calders did, however, manage to destroy many of the original family papers.

Sir John and Muriel then settled in the castle, and managed to claim other estates which had been held by the uncles. They purchased the lands of Rait from John Ogilvy of Carnousie in 1533, and in 1535 Sir John bought the Barony of Strathnairn from David, Earl of Crawford (but, before doing so, considerably reduced its value by setting fire to the Crawford seat at Daviot Castle). Surprisingly, their marriage seems to have been fairly happy, for the couple had a dozen children: six sons and six daughters. The eldest was Archibald Campbell, who succeeded to Cawdor on his father's death on 1 May 1546. He married Isabel Grant of Castle Grant. John Campbell became Bishop of the Isles, and the others established themselves on lands of their own. The daughters, too, all made good marriages. Muriel Campbell outlived her husband by almost thirty years, dying in or around 1575.

Sir Hugh Campbell (1642–1716), Fifteenth Thane of Cawdor, made considerable extensions to the castle, beginning in 1684. These included a new library, restoration of the great hall, and other domestic accommodation. He was proud of his ancestry, and incorporated over the dining-room fireplace a massive new lintel that was carved with the Campbell arms, with the initials of John Campbell and Muriel Calder on either side. There are also carvings of a weird allegorical hunting scene, perhaps telling the tale of the abduction of the heiress. Included are foxes smoking pipes, a monkey blowing a horn, a mermaid plucking a harp and a cat playing a fiddle. (The smoking foxes are an anachronism, if a reference was intended to 1510, the date of the marriage according to the lintel, for tobacco was then still undiscovered!) This lintel itself has a story behind it. Two dozen men were carrying it across the castle drawbridge on 13 April 1671 when the bridge collapsed. Fortunately no one was killed, though many, including the laird himself, were injured.

4   Chisholm of that Ilk

The Clearances of Glen Affric and Strathglass

The Highland Chisholms are actually descended from the Border clan of Chisholm of that Ilk, who owned the lands of Chisholme in Roxburghshire. Alexander Chisholm of that Ilk married Margaret of Erchless, heiress of the Aird clan, and succeeded to the chiefship in the fourteenth century. His younger brother continued the line of Chisholm in the Borders until that family died out in 1899. The Highland Chisholms owned the lands of Strathglass, and had two main seats, Comar and Erchless Castle. Our tale is one which could be repeated throughout much of the Highlands in the late eighteenth and early nineteenth centuries, when many clan chiefs found it more profitable to clear their lands of their clansmen and replace them with sheep, which required far fewer men to look after.

Alexander Chisholm, 23rd Chief of the clan, was known as An Siosal Ban, the 'fair Chisholm' (a description of his appearance – he may have had blond hair – rather than his integrity). He succeeded his father, Ruairidh, as Chief in 1785. Ruairidh had caused a number of his Chisholm tenants to emigrate when he greatly increased their rents, but Alexander was regarded as a better chief, for he granted his tenants longer (eighteen-year) leases, which gave them enough security of tenure to make it worth their while to improve their farms. However, in the late 1780s Alexander was approached by four graziers, among them Thomas Gillespie, who had a plan to rid Strathglass of its tenants and replace them with sheep. They arrived at Alexander's home of Comar, near Cannich in Strathglass, with grand-sounding figures and many proposals. Alexander's only child, his teenage daughter Mary, protested strongly to her father about the clearance of their tenants, but she was sent to her own room where she cried loudly. Later she composed herself and made her way to the kitchen, where she called together the servants of the house and explained to them what was happening.

The discussions with the Chisholm lasted long into the night, and the graziers stayed overnight as his guests. However, the next morning, when Gillespie and his associates left, Chisholm still had not made up his mind. Some tales say that the main reason that Chisholm failed to agree to the proposal was that a thousand of his clansmen surrounded Comar whilst Gillespie was inside! The servants had sent word from the house, and most of the men in Strathglass made their way to Comar and demanded a meeting with their chief, which he readily agreed to. They told Alexander that the threat from sheep was the greatest threat the clan had ever faced – greater than any battle of the past, Sheriffmuir and Culloden included. Alexander acquiesced, and in the ensuing triumphant celebration was held aloft by his cheering clansmen while the Chisholm piper played a victory tune.

Alexander died in February 1793 and was greatly lamented in the glen. The chiefship passed to his half-brother, William Chisholm (d 1817). William was often in poor health, and as a result the estate came to be run by his wife, Elizabeth MacDonald, whom he married in 1795. She was a sister of Alasdair MacDonald (or MacDonell) of Glengarry, who had cleared his lands of tenants and turned them into sheepwalks, so she knew how profitable sheep-rearing could be. The Chief and his wife sent for Thomas Gillespie again, and he laid his plans before them. Again the Chisholm clansmen gathered at Comar House, but this time the Chief's decision was less welcome. The first phase of clearance on Chisholm land took place in 1801, a second followed in 1809 (when Alexander's eighteen-year leases expired) and the last occurred in 1831.

The dispossessed tenants had few options open to them, other than try and find a new home. This could either be abroad, for there were many emigrations, often forcible, to places such as Nova Scotia, Canada proper, Australia or New Zealand, or else more locally. Many single men joined the army. A few lucky farmers managed to settle for a while on the widow Chisholm's lands, but this was a short-term home. The local bard, Alasdair Og, from Guisachan, wrote verses on the clearances.

> The abode of warriors has withered away,
> The son of the Lowlander is in your place.

Eighteenth-century cottage from Western Highlands

In 1801 799 people emigrated to Pictou in Nova Scotia, many of whom came from Strathglass and neighbouring lands. The following year a further 601 left from Fort William, 128 going to Pictou, the remainder to Upper Canada. A number of Strathglass families also emigrated via Knoydart in the same year, and in 1803 480 people left Strathglass for Pictou. A good number of the emigrants died of disease on board ship, and, once ashore, those who survived were quarantined until the contagion had passed.

There were two obstacles in the way of a total clearance of the Chisholm lands – Alexander's widow and his daughter Mary. Before his death, Alexander had offered his wife the choice of either an annuity or else the rents from a couple of townships on the estate, the rights to which would pass to his heir on her death. His widow chose the latter, which meant that, for the time being, William was unable to include the townships in his clearance proposals. As a result, there was some friction between the new Chisholm and both his sister-in-law and his niece Mary, who was still championing the tenants' cause.

By 1801 Alexander Chisholm's widow Elizabeth had moved away from the estates, but a relative, Bishop Angus Chisholm, wrote to her to tell her of the clearances:

> Oh, madam, you would really feel if you only heard the pangs and
> saw the oozing tears by which I am surrounded in this once happy
> but now devastated valley of Strathglass, looking out all anxiously for
> a home without forsaking their dear valley; but it will not do, they
> must emigrate!

During the second wave of clearances, in Glen Affric in 1809,
William Chisholm tried to persuade his sister-in-law to relinquish
her rights to the rents from some farms. William MacKenzie, a
Writer to the Signet from Edinburgh, visited Elizabeth Chisholm's
home a number of times to try and persuade her to sign over the
deeds, but she refused to do so. MacKenzie realised that she was
becoming senile, however, and persisted. Although Mary Chisholm
barred him from their home, she returned from town one day to
find him compelling her mother to sign a document – she had to
remove him forcibly from the house.

William died in 1817 and was succeeded as Chief by his son
Alexander, who was highly regarded in the county and noted for 'his
eminent classical and scientific attainments.' He was also said to be
'graced and sanctified by his unostentatious and unfeigned piety',
but he continued the work of clearance where he could, extending it
to old Mrs Chisholm's lands after her death in 1826. The tenants
were allowed to remain in their farms at first, but in 1830 they were
all bidden to a meeting at the inn in Cannich, where they expected
the chief to turn up. William, however, failed to make an appearance,
sending instead his factor, who announced that no new leases were
to be offered, and that they would all have to leave their farmhouses.
Colin Chisholm, who was present at the meeting wrote:

> I leave you to imagine the bitter grief and disappointment of men
> who attended with glowing hopes in the morning, but had to tell their
> families and dependants in the evening that they could see no alter-
> native before them but the emigrant ship, and choose between the
> scorching prairies of Australia, and the icy regions of North America.

Thomas Fraser, Lord Lovat, allowed many Chisholm farmers to
settle in Glen Strathfarrar. They were moved on again about 1846,
when Strathfarrar was cleared to turn it into a deer forest, but were
given farms elsewhere on the Lovat estates.

The farms in Strathglass were cleared in 1831, and sheep replaced the cattle. One of the main sheep-farmers to take on leases here was James Laidlaw, who hailed from the Scottish Borders. (His father was William Laidlaw, a friend of Sir Walter Scott, whose shepherd was the writer James Hogg, known as the 'Ettrick Shepherd'.) One day two of the evicted Chisholm crofters tried to take Laidlaw's life. They stood high on the hillside above the road into Glen Affric and proposed to shoot him as he passed by, but they got cold feet and withdrew. Later their nerve returned and they made their way to Laidlaw's home at Lienassie House, where they spotted the sheep-farmer through a bedroom window and took a shot at him, but failed to hit him.

Alexander Chisholm died in September 1838 at the early age of 28 and was succeeded by his brother, Duncan, who in turn died in London on 14 September 1858 – the last of the direct line of chiefs. Somewhat ironically for the dispossessed clansmen, the chieftainship passed to the descendants of Mary Chisholm, who had done so much to try and prevent the clearances. She had married an Englishman named James Gooden, and their sons adopted the name Gooden-Chisholm. More recent chiefs have dropped the 'Gooden', however.

5 Colquhoun of Luss
The Philandering Chief

The lands of Luss, which lie on the west side of Loch Lomond, were in the hands of the Luss of that Ilk until the fourteenth century, when the heiress 'Fair Maid of Luss' married Sir Robert Colquhoun of that Ilk. His ancestor, Humphrey de Kilpatrick, had been granted the lands of Colquhoun around 1246 by the Earl of Lennox for his military services, and he adopted the name of his new estate as his surname. The most notable seat was Rossdhu House (now converted to an exclusive golf club), but the clan also had seats at Bannachra, Camstradden and Rossdhu castles.

A number of the Colquhoun chiefs have suffered death at the hands of others. In 1439 Sir John, the eighth Chief of Colquhoun, was killed on the island of Inchmurrin, which lies in the midst of Loch Lomond, by Lachlan MacLean and Murdoch Gibson, Highlanders who had called a meeting to try and sort out some of their differences (Colquhoun had been appointed governor of Dumbarton Castle, and as a result made many enemies among the lawless clans of the nearby Highlands). His son, also Sir John, the ninth Chief, was a distinguished politician and was appointed comptroller of the exchequer and governor of Dumbarton Castle for life. He was killed by a cannon-ball during a siege of the castle in 1489.

The 13th Chief, Sir John Colquhoun of Luss added considerably to the family lands, which he left to his nine-year old son Humphrey. When he attained the age of eighteen Humphrey was appointed Heritable Coroner of Dunbartonshire in place of Robert Graham of Knockdolian, ratified and confirmed by a charter under the Great Seal in 1583. He was a handsome young man, and as he grew up he realised that his considerable lands and fortune were an attraction to young ladies. At the age of eighteen he married Lady

Jean Cunningham, widow of the fifth Earl of Argyll and daughter of the fifth Earl of Glencairn. She only lived for a short time, dying a year later in 1584. This left Humphrey free to marry again, and he lost no time in finding a bride. In the early part of 1586 he married Jean, daughter of the future first Marquis of Hamilton, who bore him three daughters.

However, Humphrey's eye began to wander again, and it fell upon Agnes, the wife of Andrew, the fourteenth Chief of the MacFarlanes, when she travelled through the lands of Luss on the way to Dumbarton – and she later let it be known that she found him an attractive young man. Agnes MacFarlane, a keen weaver often journeyed south along Loch Lomond to a place known as Banairidh, where a weaver lived. Originally she went to buy tweeds and woollens, but latterly her supposed visits to the weaver became more regular, and lasted longer. She was in fact meeting with Sir Humphrey, and the pair had a secret affair, meeting in the woods on the side of Loch Lomond, or anywhere else they thought their tryst might go unnoticed.

In July 1592 Andrew MacFarlane discovered his wife was involved with Sir Humphrey and angrily decided to get his own back. He gathered together a number of his clansmen, as well as men from the neighbouring MacGregors (long-time enemies of the Colquhouns) for an attack. They searched the hills and glens above Luss to find the Chief, who was accompanied by some of his clansmen and a few gentlemen of the district. A bloody battle ensued, with neither side gaining a real victory. As the summer sun sank over the hills of Argyll, the MacFarlane and MacGregor forces found renewed strength and chased Sir Humphrey back to Bannachra Castle, which stands on rising ground above the Fruin Water. Although it was a few miles from where the conflict had taken place, Sir Humphrey's fear was such that he reportedly ran with the speed of a deer across hill and dale to reach it and then barred the door behind him.

According to some traditional tales handed down from father to son in Dunbartonshire, a servant of Colquhoun was unable to reach the castle in time, and found himself locked out. With the MacFarlanes on his tail he could do no better than to hide himself in a stable outhouse. When the MacFarlanes searched these buildings, before turning their attentions to the castle, he was discovered and, under the threat of torture and possible death, gave the MacFarlanes information about the layout of the castle, and how best to attack it.

Though his life was spared, his actions earned him the epithet 'Traitor Colquhoun', and many of his descendants were known by the same name.

A different account states that 'Traitor Colquhoun' did reach the castle with his chief. According to Sir William Fraser's *The Chiefs of Colquhoun and Their Country*:

> One of the servants who attended the knight was of the same surname as himself. He had been tampered with by the assailants of his master, and treacherously made him their victim. The servant, while conducting his master to his room up a winding stair of the castle, made him by preconcert a mark for the arrows of the clan who pursued him by throwing the glare of a paper torch upon his person when opposite a loophole. A winged arrow, darted from its string with a steady aim, pierced the unhappy knight to the heart, and he fell dead on the spot. The fatal loophole is still pointed out, but the stair, like its unfortu- · nate lord, has crumbled into dust.

A fire arrow set the roof of the tower alight, and the traitor opened the iron door, allowing the MacFarlanes to enter. One of them cut Colquhoun's head from his body, whilst another withdrew his dirk and emasculated the chief.

According to an old account of the incident, 'so little regard did these savage freebooters pay to the laws of chivalry that they brutally violated the person of Jean Colquhoun, the fair and helpless daughter of Sir Humphrey'; she must have been little more than five years old at the time. As a final gesture before leaving Inveruglas Castle, one of the MacFarlane clansmen took the chief's wife a wooden bowl, covered by a cloth, containing the chief of Colquhoun's genitals, which he presented to her. 'This is your share of the spoils,' he said. 'You will understand yourself what it is.' (Some accounts state that the clansman went further – he cooked the bowl's contents and served them to her at dinner.)

According to a number of accounts of the altercation, it was none other than Sir Humphrey's younger brother, John (or Iain), who was responsible for letting the MacFarlanes know of the Chief's affair. The two neighbouring clans had long been at feud with each other, and the affair probably enraged the Colquhouns and the MacFarlanes alike. This was alleged in Birrel's *Diary* to be the reason why John, the second son of Sir John, did not succeed to Luss on Sir Humphrey's death, the chiefship passing to the third son, Alexander.

It has also been alleged that it was John himself who shot the arrow which killed his brother. John was known to have been a greedy character, and he realised full well that, if his brother died without any sons, he himself would succeed to the estates. John Colquhoun was beheaded at the Mercat Cross in Edinburgh on 30 November 1592 for killing his brother.

6 Farquharson of Inverey
The Black Colonel

The Farquharson clan are a branch of the Shaws of Rothiemurchus, taking their name from one of that family's younger sons, Fearchair, or Farquhar, who was the forester to the Earl of Mar in the fifteenth century. The MacFhearchair, or Farquharson family, became a clan in its own right, remaining part of the Clan Chattan confederation even though their lands were located across the Monadh Ruadh mountains. The main branches were Inverey, Finzean and Invercauld – the last-named being regarded at present as the chiefly line, although the original chiefs were the Inverey branch. The swap came about in the eighteenth century, when John of Invercauld claimed that his branch had become involved in the 1715 uprising unwittingly, whereas Colonel Patrick of Inverey had been a leader in the rising, and was attainted for his part in it.

Our tale concerns Colonel Patrick's father, John Farquharson, third Laird of Inverey. His home, Inverey Castle, stood at Inverey village, five miles west of Braemar in Aberdeenshire, and the old Gallows Tree grew in front of the ruins for many years before a gravel pit undermined its roots and killed it. He married Marjorie Leith, daughter of George Leith of Overhall, by whom he had a number of children, among them Patrick, Charles and James. Farquharson, who was said to summon his servants to the table by firing off a pistol, was better known by his nickname, the 'Black Colonel', or An Coirneal Dubh, from his dark-coloured hair and swarthy complexion. A number of his belongings survive at the seat of the present chief, Invercauld House; these include his broadsword and targe, the latter pitted by bullet holes. It is related that, when he required the assistance of his chief retainer (a man named Alasdair MacDougall), he shot his pistol at this targe, and the sound it made resounded through the castle and was heard by MacDougall.

Farquharson first came to prominence on 7 September 1666 when he killed John Gordon of Braickley and several others in a skirmish that resulted from a cattle-rustling incident in which sixteen cows were stolen. This was the last of several conflicts between the two families, including a dispute over the taking of salmon from the River Dee out of season, in which Gordon acted on behalf of the city of Aberdeen. After the theft of the cattle, the Black Colonel and some of his men went to Braickley house (near Ballater), demanding that Gordon came out and settled their differences. Gordon, outnumbered, was unwilling to fight, but his wife goaded him into action. After his death, it is said that Gordon's wife entertained the Farquharsons in Braickley house, causing great scandal in the county. An old ballad recounts:

> Inverey came down Deeside, whistlin' an' playin',
> He was at braw Braickley's gates, ere it was dawin'.

Farquharson was summoned before the court in Edinburgh to answer for his part in the murders but, as a result of the intervention of the Chief of Clan Chattan, no accusers turned up to give evidence, so John Farquharson was allowed to go free.

He had to lie low for a time, however, and a number of his hideouts are still pointed out on Deeside to this day. One was a mile and a half up Glen Ey from his castle. The Ey Burn tumbles through a rocky defile, and here there is a hidden rock shelf, little more than a flat recess in a cliff-face, which is known as the Colonel's Bed. It is said that 'he was not always without agreeable company' in this hideout, and locals are known to point out a large flat rock which was his 'table', and a depression which held water was his 'basin'. Nearer to Inverey is the Colonel's Cave, located on the east side of Creag a' Chait, overlooking Inverey Castle.

John Farquharson was a Jacobite and supported John Graham of Claverhouse ('Bonnie Dundee' as he became known), but his near neighbour the Earl of Mar was a supporter of King William, and the difference in allegiance of the two families caused considerable strife in Deeside. Farquharson went south with Dundee and fought at the Battle of Bothwell Bridge, where his conduct was so memorable that some years later Graham appointed him a colonel on account of the ability he had shown at Bothwell. He raised an army of Farquharsons who were to fight for Dundee.

Braemar Castle

In April 1689 General Hugh Mackay of Scourie sent a party of fifty dragoons and sixty foot, under the Master of Forbes, to occupy Braemar Castle on behalf of King William. The Black Colonel led his men under the cover of darkness towards Braemar. They ascended the steep sides of Creag Choinnich, which rises above the castle, and from it fired musket shots into the night. Awakening to the sound of gunfire, the soldiers within were terrified by the thought of death, and made their way back down the glen as fast as they could, whereupon Farquharson's men looted the castle and set it alight.

The battle of Killiecrankie on 17 July 1689 saw a turnaround in the fortunes of the two sides; although the Jacobites won, their leader Dundee was killed; his leadership was missed, and the Jacobite revolt quickly crumbled. The Black Colonel had to hide in the district after this, his hideout known to many but revealed by none. One of his faithful clanswomen, Annie Ban, or 'Annie the fair' made the journey each night to supply him with food and other necessities. According to an old tale, one time when the redcoats came to Inverey looking for Farquharson, he was asleep in bed. Awakened by one of his servants, he ran naked from the castle, but the soldiers spotted him and pursued at speed. Farquharson ran towards the Ey Burn and, at a rocky part of the burn, jumped across the spate-swollen waters, eluding his pursuers. Later a bridge was erected here and named Drochaid an Leum, or 'bridge of the leap', to commemorate the event.

On another occasion an old woman from Braemar arrived at Inverey to warn the Colonel that the redcoats were once again heading that way to try to capture him. Farquharson managed to escape up Glen Ey, leaving behind a few retainers who held up the soldiers for a short while. At one point a cloaked figure emerged from the castle and ran like a hare away from the building; the soldiers gave chase and caught the figure, but found that rather than the Colonel, they had captured none other than Annie Ban, acting as a decoy. The redcoats returned to the castle and, in disgust at being eluded once more, set the building on fire.

The Black Colonel was nearly captured on a number of other occasions, but he managed to pull off some rather daring escapes which have become the stuff of legend. One day a party of redcoats came across him riding in the Pass of Ballater and at once gave chase. Farquharson decided that the only possible way of making a getaway was to head straight up the precipitous side of the pass. The route was rocky and of unsure footing, but his horse managed to climb the precipice, and he escaped. This ascent has ever since been known as the Race of Tullich.

In August 1690 the Black Colonel besieged Abergeldie Castle but was unable to take it, so his men surrounded the tower and settled down to starve the government soldiers out. However, General Mackay and Colonel Livingstone managed to relieve them just in time; according to Mackay the castle would have had to surrender in another three days. Mackay then went on, 'to terrify others from like attempts, I burned twelve miles of a very fertile Highland country and at least twelve or fourteen hundred houses. I left order to permit none to rebuild but by delivering up their arms and swearing allegiance to their Majesties William and Mary.'

The Black Colonel died around 1698. He had long wished to be buried with his ancestors at the ancient kirkyard of St Maurice at Inverey, but for some reason his wishes were not followed, and his corpse was laid to rest at St Andrew's kirkyard in Braemar. The day after the burial, the locals were amazed to discover that his coffin had seemingly disinterred itself. A party of men hastily reinterred the Colonel, but two days later the coffin again appeared above ground. Someone then remembered the Colonel's wish to be laid to rest at Inverey, and the disinterments were seen as a sign that he was unhappy with his resting place. A group of family members arranged for the coffin to be rafted up the River Dee to Inverey, where he was finally buried. The coffin lay at peace for a number of years until a couple of gravediggers, preparing for another burial, accidentally broke it open. As a memento of the Colonel, each sexton took a tooth from his skull. Later that night it is said that the ghost of Farquharson himself appeared before the two men, warning them to return the teeth. The frightened gravediggers replaced them the following day.

Braemar Castle was sequestered from the Jacobite Earl of Mar, and, though in ruins, was purchased in 1732 by John Farquharson, ninth Laird of Invercauld. It was restored in 1748 and remains in Farquharson hands to this day.

7   Forbes of that Ilk
Feuds and Fish

The great clan Forbes has its homeland in the fertile countryside of Aberdeenshire – in particular alongside the River Don, where the family built a great number of castles. According to tradition, the first chief of the clan, Ochonochar, slew a savage bear which roamed this countryside, rendering it uninhabitable, and then claimed the Braes of Forbes for himself. In 1272 the chief had a new feudal charter granted to him by Alexander III (previously the land was held 'under God'), and Sir Alexander, the eighth Chief, was created Lord Forbes by James II in 1442. The present chief, the 23rd Lord Forbes, still owns Castle Forbes and surrounding estate.

Our tale relates to John, the 13th laird, and 6th Lord Forbes, who lived in the sixteenth century. He seems to have been a rather obstinate person, who flouted authority and often took the law into his own hands. John Forbes was the third son of William, third Lord Forbes, who died in 1483. His two elder brothers, Alexander and Arthur, succeeded to the barony in turn, but they both died young and without issue, so John succeeded sometime in 1493. He married, successively Lady Catherine Stewart, daughter of the Earl of Atholl, Christian Lundin and Elizabeth Barlow.

In 1527 Lord Forbes was one of a number of Highland barons who was given the right to exterminate members of Clan Chattan, which, under William Mackintosh, its 15th Chief, had attacked lands in Moray. A Royal proclamation was issued which allowed Lord Forbes and others to 'invaid thame to thair vter destructioun, be slauchtir, byrning, drouning, and vther wayis: and leif na creatur levand of that clann, except preistis, wemen, and barnis'. This commission appealed to Lord Forbes, but he and the other barons were unwilling to carry it out on account of its severity.

In October 1530 Lord Forbes was indicted to the justiciary court at Dundee, along with his son, the Master of Forbes, and a few others. They were charged with the slaughter of Alexander Seton of Meldrum, the result of an Aberdeenshire feud. The Master was fortunate enough to receive remission under the great seal, but Lord Forbes seems not to have attended, and seventeen landed gentlemen were fined bail for not ensuring his attendance. In July 1532 Lord Forbes received a fresh charter to his lands under the Great Seal.

Yet another feud, against the Gordons, lasted over ten years. It originated over the acquisition of some church lands, and both parties were regularly called before the court to pay fines as surety of good behaviour. On 29 July 1533 Lord Forbes, his sons John and William and a relative, William Forbes of Corsindae, were called before Aberdeen justiciary court and had to find security to ensure that they attended the next sitting to face a charge of destroying property belonging to the Gordons. They had made their way under the cover of darkness to the Earl of Huntly's farm and burned wooden sheep-pens before disappearing once more into the night. The Forbeses were called to the court three years later to find caution money once more.

In 1536 a charge of treason against King James V was levelled at both Lord Forbes and his son. The charge was brought before the king and Privy Council, by George Gordon, Earl of Huntly, using the strength of the law to continue the family feud. Using the evidence of an 'unprincipled' man, John Strachan – who had been refused favour by the Forbeses, and thus went to their enemies instead – he claimed that the two Forbeses had conspired to take His Majesty's life and destroy his army at Jedburgh, in the Scottish borders. They were both arrested in December and taken south to Edinburgh Castle, where they were locked up in the traitors' cells.

After a lengthy confinement Lord Forbes was put on trial, but no evidence of any treasonable behaviour was discovered, and all charges against him were dropped. He was allowed to go free. The Master of Forbes protested his innocence, and offered to fight Lord Huntly in a duel, something which was legal under the old feudal laws. The Privy Council, however, did not authorise this, but asked Huntly to subscribe a bond of 30,000 merks to make good his accusation. The Master was tried on 14 July 1537 at the Court of Justiciary in Edinburgh. He was found guilty as charged, and ordered to be drawn on a hurdle down the High Street of the capital and then hanged on the gallows; as a traitor, his corpse was to be quartered. Three days later the first part of the sentence was carried out, but 'as a favour' to save his family from embarrassment, he was beheaded by the 'maiden' (a type of guillotine) instead of being hanged. Before his execution took place, the Master told the assembled crowd that not one of the charges he was to die for was established satisfactorily, and that the judges who had convicted him of the crime had all been bribed by Lord Huntly. He protested his innocence of the treason charge, but said that he was willing to die as a punishment for the murder of Seton of Meldrum.

In the early sixteenth century the citizens of Aberdeen seemed likely to lose their rights to the river fishing within their city. The matter was of serious concern, and had been in dispute for some time. Lord Forbes – who at that time lived at Putachie Castle, site of the present Castle Forbes – took up the cause on behalf of the citizens and managed to win the case in the High Courts. The Aberdonians were extremely grateful to Lord Forbes for saving the rights and persuaded their magistrates to reward him. It was agreed that he was to receive a tun (or 252 gallons) of wine from the city on an annual basis. However, Lord Forbes seems to have spent some days fishing the River Don 'in indue time' – that is, out of season. This greatly annoyed the city magistrates, who decided that the gift of claret should be withdrawn. They also decided that no pension should be payable to Lord Forbes, or any other person, for keeping the waters, and that any future such pension would be classed as 'black mail'.

Forbes was upset at this decision, for he regarded the wine as his by right. In 1530 he gathered a band of his clansmen, dressed them in traditional Highland garb, and armed them with broadswords and muskets. This wild bunch of Highland caterans then rode into the city and frightened the citizens. The dispute was settled amicably, however. Lord Forbes and his followers left Aberdeen without their horses or arms, and in 1595 his grandson, John, eighth Lord Forbes, built himself a new town house in Aberdeen. The magistrates agreed to furnish him with over one hundred merks worth of materials for this, as a remembrance of his keeping of the waters of the Dee and Don, 'fra slayeris of blak fishe in forbidden tyme, as the said lordis predicessoris did obefoir to this burgh'.

The sixth Lord Forbes died in 1547, and the title passed to his eldest surviving son, William, but the Gordon feud still rumbled on. Lesser branches of the two families behaved just as bloodily. Henry Gordon, the laird of Knock Castle, near Ballater, was killed in a

Forbes raid on his tower some time during their feud of 1571–5. His successor's seven sons were cutting peats one day on Forbes land when Alexander Forbes of Strathgirnock came upon them and slew them all, decapitating them and tying their heads to the shafts of their 'flauchter-spads', or peat spades. When Gordon of Knock discovered that all his sons had been killed he was so upset that he fell down the spiral stair of his own castle, broke his neck and died. 'Black' Alasdair Gordon of Abergeldie attacked Strathgirnock house and killed Forbes in retribution, hanging him from his own rafters.

At Perth in 1582 an agreement was reached between the Gordons and the Forbes, and it was decreed that Lord Forbes and 46 other members of the clan were to be exempt from Huntly's jurisdiction in the north. The two clans were also brought together in 1558 when John (afterwards the eighth Lord Forbes) married the Earl of Huntly's eldest daughter, Margaret. The feud may have continued, however, for the pair divorced in 1574!

8   Fraser of Lovat
Field of the Shirts

The Frasers originated in the south of Scotland, where they had a number of castles in Upper Tweeddale, but in the thirteenth century they acquired lands in the north of the country and have since become more associated with the Highlands. There are two main branches of the clan, the Frasers of Lovat and the Frasers of Saltoun, and, though the latter are regarded as the more senior, the two families are classed as separate clans.

Around 1460 Hugh Fraser was created Lord Lovat, or Lord Fraser of Lovat. The subject of our tale is his grandson, also Hugh, the third Lord Lovat. He did much to extend the family estates, receiving charters to various lands in Inverness-shire, and in 1528 he received permission from King James V to build himself a fortified house, complete with dungeon and iron doors. In 1539 he resigned the title of his estates to the crown, receiving from the monarch a grant of a barony, passable to heirs male whatsoever, failing which heirs whatsoever. In 1542 he obtained from James V a further charter to the lands of Beaufort, which have been associated with the clan until recent years.

In 1544 the chiefship of the Clanranald MacDonalds was in dispute, as it had been since the death of Alasdair MacDonald in 1530. There were a number of claimants, including Lord Lovat's nephew Ronald Gallda, or 'the stranger', son of Donald Glass of Moidart. He is said to have been the legitimate claimant. The MacDonalds themselves had appointed Ronald's cousin, John Moidartach MacDonald, or Iain Muydertach (d 1584), as their chief.

Lord Lovat led the Frasers into Moidart and attacked the MacDonalds, assisting his sister's son in reclaiming his right. The MacDonalds, however, were unwilling to accept Ronald as their chief, and evicted him from Castle Tioram. The MacDonalds and Camerons then raided the lands of Glenelg, Strathglass and Abertarf, which belonged to the Frasers, destroying many of the houses and stealing cattle. They also raided Glen Urquhart and took Urquhart Castle – among the booty taken back to Moidart were 1,500 cattle, 2,000 sheep, 300 horses, 1,000 lambs, 1,500 goats and oats and barley. These lands the MacDonalds and Camerons proposed keeping for themselves 'in all time coming'.

The Earl of Arran, Governor of the kingdom, was notified of the disturbances on the west coast of Scotland and appointed the Marquis of Huntly as Lieutenant of the Highlands. Lord Lovat gathered four hundred of his clan together and persuaded Huntly to join him in crushing the other factions and appointing Ronald as chief. The Gordons and Frasers marched down through the Great Glen towards Inverlochy, and from there cut across Moidart to Castle Tioram, the seat of Clanranald. The castle was easily taken, and Ronald was again established as the chief in Moidart; an old account states that the Frasers and Grants chased the MacDonalds into 'their awan cuntrye apoun the west seis, quhair Lawland men cuid haif no acces unto thame'.

On the return march the Gordons and Frasers split their forces at Gloy, overlooking Loch Lochy, the Marquis of Huntly taking his men back to Aberdeenshire. Huntly had offered to accompany the Frasers back north, but it was thought the MacDonalds were now defeated, and that the Gordon soldiers were no longer required. Things could not have been further from the truth; the MacDonalds had been stealthily following their enemies back through the Great Glen, keeping hidden in the distance. Their force comprised the Clanranald MacDonalds and the MacDonells of Glengarry, along with members of Clan Cameron, including the 13th Chief, Ewen MacAllan Cameron, and his grandson and successor Ewen Beag. They knew it was pointless and potentially lethal to attack the combined forces of Huntly and Lovat, since these outnumbered them considerably, but, once the Gordons had left, the MacDonalds had a greater chance. They continued to stalk the Frasers through the Great Glen, all the while planning the best time to attack.

Three miles further north, near Letterfinlay, Lord Lovat became aware that he was being followed. He sent one of his trusted clans-men, Iain Cleireach, with fifty men to secure an important pass and prevent the MacDonalds from cutting the Fraser route home, but for some unknown reason, Iain Cleireach was unable to accomplish this.

At the northern end of Loch Lochy was a wide stretch of marshy bogland, and here the MacDonalds decided to make their move. They descended from the hillside above Kilfinan, on the west side of the bog, their screaming war-cries resounding through the glen; in total they numbered around five hundred, divided into seven companies. Blocked in by the surrounding landscape, Lord Lovat decided to face the MacDonalds, rather than make a quick exit to the north (for the Frasers were within striking distance of their homeland). This was to be a great mistake, for, having only three hundred men, he was outnumbered.

It was the 3rd July, and the battle took place in the warmth of the midday sun. The fighting was so hard that all the clansmen were sweating in the heat, and most of them were forced to take off their feileadh mor, or great kilts, and fight wearing only their undergarments or shirts. As a result the battle was known by the Highlanders as Blàr na Leine, or the 'field of shirts', although other writers refer to it as the Battle of Loch Lochy.

At first the battle was fought with bows and arrows, the two clans keeping some distance apart. A number of men on both sides were killed, and this phase lasted until all the arrows were broken or lost. The surviving clansmen then drew their swords, Lochaber axes and dirks and engaged each other at close quarters. A contemporary account noted that 'they were felled down on each side like trees in a wood till room was made by these breaches and at last all came to fight hand and fist.' No side could really claim to have won, for the battle became a fight to the end, rather than a fight for victory, and it was only the fall of darkness that brought it to an end. The number killed was considerable, with both sides losing hundreds of men – although the tradition that only four Frasers and ten MacDonalds survived is probably rather suspect.

Among the many dead was Lord Lovat. It was noted that he made great headway in the struggle, hacking his way through the opposition with his great claymore. At length a MacDonald managed to fell him, and his clansmen rejoiced when they heard that 'Thuit an cruaidh chascar' ('the sturdy slasher is fallen'). His corpse was later recovered from the marsh, taken back to the Fraser homeland and buried in the priory at Beauly. An old tombstone, still to be seen in the priory and reckoned to be Hugh's, depicts him wearing armour, his hands clasped in prayer. According to the Wardlaw Manuscript:

This great and good man [was] gathered to his fathers in the 55 yeare of his age, his worth and vertues truely such that he was very much lamented even by his very enemies, for besides the splendor of his ancestry and the statliness, bravery, and comeliness of his personage, he was master of a great deal of wit, and singular prudence, providence, and provesse in very troublesom times. His authority and conduct in his great trust reacht farr, his intelligence farr and neare wonderfull, none could surprise his country without an allarum; he could read men as bookes, could not abid baseness, had a great esteem for men of integrity and spirit though never so mean, being himselfe a man of undoubted vallour and currage.

James Fraser, Lord Lovat's brother, was also killed in battle, leaving behind a wife and young daughter. Lovat's heir, Simon, the Master of Lovat (only recently returned from France, where he was receiving his education, when he became involved in the feud), was mortally wounded and captured by the MacDonalds, dying three days later as their prisoner. Unmarried, he too was buried at Beauly. The title passed to his half-brother, Alexander, who was then only seventeen years old. There is a tradition that the Frasers of Lovat would have been almost totally wiped out after this battle, but for the fact that in the Fraser lands around Beauly eighty wives were carrying children at the time and, when they gave birth, all the offspring were boys.

9 Galbraith of Culcreuch
The Fugitive Chief

The country of the Galbraiths lies on what may be termed the southern extremity of the Highlands. They were known as Clann a' Bhreatannaich, or the British clan, having settled here from north Wales in the twelfth century. Their seat, Culcreuch Castle, stands in its parkland to the north of the Stirlingshire village of Fintry. The last real chief to stay there died in exile, frightened to return home after being denounced as a rebel. The castle is now a hotel, but the original sixteenth-century tower, with its vaulted bar and haunted bedrooms, is still a major part of the building.

It is said that a visitor to the castle in 1582 was murdered in what is known as the Chinese Bird Room (from the pattern on its wallpaper) in the original keep. Whether or not Robert Galbraith, the chief we are looking at, was involved in this is unknown, but it must have happened in his lifetime, for he was born sometime in the middle of the sixteenth century. He seems at first to have been an upstanding citizen, for he is on record as being the Sheriff Depute of Dumbarton in March 1597. Since Culcreuch lands are in the Fintry Hills, on the boundary between the Highlands and Lowlands, the Galbraiths were regarded as being more civilized than the true Highland clans, and Robert Galbraith was employed by the government to help quell the rebel clans – in particular the MacGregors and the MacAulays. In 1592 he received a commission from the crown to pursue the Clan Gregor (which family was to be proscribed in 1603, after which no one could bear the name MacGregor, and it was perfectly legal to kill anyone by that name). When Robert's father died his widow, to her son's displeasure, married Aulay MacAulay of Ardincaple, chief of that clan. The MacAulays had long regarded themselves as cadets of the Clan Gregor, so Robert used his commission of fire and sword against the MacGregors to annoy MacAulay, who died in 1617.

Culcreuch Castle and Galbraith Arms

Galbraith got himself seriously into debt, in particular to his brother-in-law, Alexander Seton of Gargunnock. He reckoned that the only real way of clearing his debt without selling his estate was to kill Seton. Therefore, as Seton was passing along a country road one day, Galbraith led a group of cloaked men up to his coach and surrounded it. Seton feared that they were a group of highwaymen, but his party was not held up nor robbed. A shot was fired into the coach, although it missed Seton, and, thinking that their task was complete, the masked men rode away.

Robert Galbraith was denounced as a rebel, and an order for his arrest was issued in 1622. However, he fled from justice, escaping across the North Channel to Ireland, where he spent the rest of his days. (He seems to have died sometime before 1642.) Robert's son was left at home, but he inherited nothing of his father's estate, for in 1624 Culcreuch was given to Robert's brother-in-law Alexander Seton of Gargunnock in payment of some of the debts. Alexander disposed of the estate in 1632 to Robert Napier, a second son of Napier of Merchiston. Robert Galbraith's grandson, James, the 19th Chief of the Galbraiths, who died without any family, was the last known chief of the clan.

10 Gordon of Huntly
The Many Feuds

The Gordons originated in the Border county of Berwickshire, where there is a parish and village of the name. In 1333 Sir Adam Gordon was granted the lordship of Strathbogie in Aberdeenshire by Robert the Bruce, and the clan's principal seat then became Strathbogie Castle. In 1506 Alexander Gordon, third Earl of Huntly, received a charter confirming his lands, which stated that his castle, 'which was formerly called Strathbogie, be in all future times named the Castle of Huntly'. The ruins of this are now preserved by Historic Scotland. The Gordon chiefs were often in the thick of any troubles that took place in the Highlands, being at feud with the Campbell, Forbes, Murray and other clans.

One of the most troublesome chiefs was George Gordon, sixth Earl of Huntly, who was born sometime in the middle of the sixteenth century and succeeded as Chief in 1576. He was a great favourite of James VI and received many honours from him. Gordon rebuilt his castle of Huntly, made many improvements to his lands and erected a new castle at Ruthven in Badenoch, on the site of the present ruinous Hanoverian barracks. The building of this castle, on what was Gordon's hunting territory, was seen as a slight by the Clan Chattan, who feared Huntly was trying to overawe their clan. As they were actually the earl's vassals and tenants, they were due to supply him with materials for building the castle, but the Mackintoshes refused to do so, thus beginning a feud with the Gordons.

In the late sixteenth century many of the Highlanders distrusted the power of the Gordons of Huntly, whom they derisively named the 'Cocks of the North'. A plot was hatched by the Chief of Grant and Sir John Campbell of Cawdor which was to result in Huntly

George Gordon, first Marquis of Huntly, and Huntly Castle

falling foul of the law. One James Gordon went to Ballindalloch Castle to help his aunt collect money that was due to her but had been misappropriated by the tutor at Ballindalloch, John Grant. Most of the money was collected, but a few dues remained unpaid; this resulted in a brawl at the castle, with servants from both sides fighting. At a later date John Gordon, brother of Gordon of Cluny Castle, married the Ballindalloch widow, upsetting the tutor, who murdered one of his servants. As a result Gordon managed to get the Grants outlawed and called upon the Earl of Huntly, as his chief, to arrest them. Huntly besieged Ballindalloch on 2 November 1590, but the tutor escaped.

Cawdor and Grant then set about bringing their plot into action. They persuaded Lachlan Mor Mackintosh, 16th Chief of that clan, along with the Earl of Atholl and the Earl of Moray to join them in a campaign against Huntly. Moray was easily persuaded to take up arms, for he had long harboured a desire to be as strong as Huntly in the north, and saw this as an ideal time to make his mark. The group met at Forres to lay their plans, but Huntly got wind of the meeting and rode with all haste to the town. The faction left Forres behind and fled to Moray's Darnaway Castle. Huntly pursued them, but most of the chiefs fled for the moors, leaving only the Earl of Moray behind. Huntly sent John Gordon ahead to spy on the castle, but he was spotted from the battlements and shot by one of Moray's servants.

Huntly decided that the castle could not easily be taken by force, so he retreated and set off for Edinburgh, where he persuaded Chancellor Maitland to give him a commission of fire and sword against the Earl of Moray, which allowed him to attack the Earl under the laws of the country. He also sent a force under Allan MacDonald Dubh, 16th Chief of Clan Cameron, to attack the Mackintoshes and Clan Chattan. This killed 'XLI [41] of Macintoshes and XXIII [23] tennents of Grant, and hurte the Larde of Balendalough'.

When Lord Moray was staying at his Fife house of Donibristle, and Huntly was in Edinburgh, the latter saw this as an ideal time to take action. He sent Captain John Gordon to ask the Earl to capitulate, but he refused, and a shot was fired from the house which wounded Gordon. His forces then attacked the house, setting it alight and forcing an entry. Although Huntly had told them to take Moray alive, the laird of Cluny, whose brother was killed at Darnaway, and the laird of Gight, whose brother had just been wounded, pursued the Earl and caught him on the shore. They killed him with a number of slashes to his body. A painting of the wounds received still hangs in Darnaway Castle's great hall.

Clan Chattan rose up to avenge the Earl's death and invaded Gordon countryside. They spoiled much of the land around Glenmuick and Strathdee, killing four men, one of them the very respected old laird of Breaghly, or Braickley, near Ballater. He had invited the rebels into his house, suspecting nothing, and plied them with kind hospitality. Treacherously, the Clan Chattan men killed him in his own home.

Incensed at this, Huntly led a force into the parish of Petty, which lies between Inverness and Nairn, home of the Mackintoshes, where he killed many people and laid waste the countryside, carrying off hundreds of Mackintosh cattle and dividing them among his followers. Simultaneously, a force of 800 Clan Chattan soldiers under

William Mackintosh, son of Lachlan Mor Mackintosh, was in Huntly's lands of Cabrach doing the same thing. The two forces actually met up at a spot known as Staplie- or Steeplegate, where the Gordons defeated Clan Chattan, killing 60 of their finest men and wounding William their leader. Lord Huntly then went to Petty a second time and, with the assistance of the forces under Alexander Gordon of Abergeldie and Clanranald soldiers, laid waste the lands of Mackintosh and Grant, killing many.

In October 1594 Huntly was involved in the 'Spanish Blanks' plot, which was seen as an invitation to the Spanish authorities to invade Scotland, where they would receive the support of the Roman Catholic earls of Huntly, Angus and Errol, amongst others. Huntly having thus been forfeited by Parliament, the Earl of Argyll, chief of the Campbells, was appointed His Majesty's Lieutenant in the north of Scotland in his place. Argyll proceeded to lead a large force of 12,000 men north to avenge the death of his brother-in-law Lord Moray. With him were clansmen under the Earl of Tullibardine (heir of the chief of the Murrays), Sir Lachlan Maclean of Duart, Lachlan Mor Mackintosh, John Grant (13th Chief), Alasdair MacGregor (11th Chief), Ruaridh MacNeil of Barra (15th Chief), and many others.

The western clansmen at first attacked Ruthven Castle, in Strathspey, but it was too heavily guarded by Huntly's supporters, the MacPhersons, so they gave up and turned their attention to the east. Meanwhile another large group of clansmen had been brought out by their chiefs from all over Aberdeenshire and beyond in the campaign against Huntly. These included the eighth Lord Forbes, the Frasers, the Dunbars, MacKenzies, Irvines, Ogilvys, Leslies and Munros. Huntly, who could only raise his own men, as well as those under Lord Errol, had a much smaller force of around 1,500; he sent a party of scouts to spy on the enemy – who by chance had done the same. The two advance parties met, and Huntly's men managed to kill all but one of the opponent's spies. This was seen as a good omen to the Gordons, and they sniffed a greater victory to follow.

The two main forces met on the Braes of Glenlivet on Thursday 3 October 1594. Argyll was surprised that Huntly's smaller army was willing to fight, especially when Argyll held the upper ground, which was steep and rocky. Huntly's men were all mounted, and at first had to ride over the mossy ground at the foot of the slope before they could reach the enemy, most of whom were on foot. A shot from the Gordon side killed Ruaridh MacNeil, and his clansmen lost direction thereafter. Huntly decided this was the time to charge, which he did successfully (at one point Huntly's horse was shot from beneath him, but a second was quickly procured for him). His uncle, Sir Patrick Gordon of Auchindoun, was killed, but the Gordons fought all the harder, as if trying to avenge his death.

Argyll's men began to tire, and many of them fled the battlefield. The Grants and their Chief defected from the left wing of his army and joined the Gordons. Lachlan Maclean was left in front, but, soon realising that he seemed to be fighting alone, he ordered his men to retire and made a hasty escape. The Gordons pursued the fleeing soldiers as far as the Allt a' Choileachain, after which the hillside was too steep for mounted soldiers. In all, the Campbell forces lost over 700 men, the Gordons only fifteen.

Huntly's foes subsequently attacked his castle, using gunpowder which had been granted to them by the Aberdeen authorities, and the old fifteenth-century tower was virtually destroyed. Huntly fled the country, passing through Germany, France and Flanders, and remained in exile for a year and five months until the king summoned him back to Scotland. He settled his differences with the king in 1597, and two years later the monarch created him the first Marquis of Huntly. To settle the feuds which had cost so many lives, a series of marriages were arranged to bring the families closer together. Argyll's eldest daughter married Lord George Gordon, later the second Marquis of Huntly, and Lady Anne, Huntly's daughter, married James Stewart, the heir of the Bonnie Earl who was slain at Donibristle.

Huntly's time abroad gave him some ambitious plans for his castle, and as a result the extremely fine heraldic doorway and oriel window frieze on the palace block of Huntly Castle was constructed, some of the finest masonry work of its day. Inside the palace he erected a number of grand fireplaces, one of which incorporates stone medallions depicting both himself and his wife, Henrietta Stewart.

Lord Huntly received further honours from the king, including the Earldom of Enzie, Viscountcy of Inverness and Lordships of Badenoch, Lochaber, Strathavon, Auchindoun, Balmore, Garthie and Kincardine. He died in 1636.

II Grant of that Ilk
James of the Forays

Clan Grant is one of the oldest clans in Scotland, though its origin is in dispute. Some say that it was a very early branch of the MacGregors, both being members of the great Clan Alpin, whereas others claim the Grants are descendants of the ancient king Kenneth MacAlpine (d 860), and a third theory is that they are of Norman descent. In any case, they have been settled on the northern side of the Grampian Mountains, in particular in Strathspey, Glen Urquhart, and around Loch Ness, from the earliest of times.

The seat of the Grants in the fifteenth century was the castle of Freuchie, which stood north of Grantown on Spey. The castle was renamed Castle Grant in 1694, and the Barony of Freuchie became the Regality of Grant. The first Grant of Freuchie was Sir Duncan Grant (d 1475), but our story concerns his great, great grandson, James Grant, 11th Chief of that Ilk, who was born in the latter part of the fifteenth century, and succeeded his father, Iain nam Bard Ruadh, or 'Red John the Poet' around 1528. During his father's lifetime, James had been a signatory to an Indenture made on 22 October 1520 between the Grants and the Camerons of Lochiel, following the marriage of James's sister, Agnes Grant, to Donald Cameron (d 1538), son of Ewen Cameron, 13th Chief of that clan. It stated that each member would 'stand till vder in leil, trew, anefald, kyndnes manteinans and defendoris of vderis for all the dais of thair lieffis ... ilkane to defend vderis in thair personis, gudis, landis, possessionis, kin, frendis, party, and auherdans, in all thair actionis and querelis'.

James was responsible for making a number of alterations to Castle Grant in 1536, extending the old tower. However, the Grant clan was a troublesome one during the time of James's chiefship. He

Castle Grant

was a noted raider, known by his contemporaries as Seumas nan Creach, or 'James of the Forays', and renowned for his willingness to undertake any warlike dare; his stature and skill were such that he was usually capable of performing them.

A feud within the clan arose out of the murder of his kinsman, John Grant of Ballindalloch. Although this was the work of John Roy Grant of Carron, the natural son of John Grant of Glenmoriston, it had been instigated by James Grant, who had a grievance against the laird of Ballindalloch because of an incident which took place at Elgin Fair. Grant of Ballindalloch attacked Thomas Grant in the street, whereupon his brother James murdered Ballindalloch. James went into hiding, refused to stand trial on the appointed day and was denounced as an outlaw. James tried a number of times to bring the two branches of the clan together to settle their differences amicably, but these efforts came to naught. The feud passed from father to son in the two families for years and resulted in yet more deaths in 1628, when John Grant of Ballindalloch killed John Grant of Carron.

In 1545, after their victory at Blar na Leine (see Chapter 8), the Captain of Clanranald MacDonald and the Camerons of Lochiel attacked the Grant estates on the west side of Loch Ness, taking James's Urquhart Castle and plundering much of the glen. A list of items stolen from the castle makes interesting reading: feather beds, complete with bolsters, blankets and sheets, pots and pans, a kist containing £300 Scots, roasting spits, brewing vats, doors, gates, tables, chairs, guns, powder and armour. Urquhart Castle was subsequently restored by James Grant.

Though warlike, James was an adherent of the royal house and a supporter of Mary Queen of Scots. He signed the bond against what he described 'our auld enymyies of Ingland'. Mary's father King James V had been an admirer of James Grant and often called upon him to use his skill and might to keep the surrounding clans in order. A letter from him was long preserved by the family:

> ... praying and charging him, with his kin, friends and partakers to pass with his Lieutenant-General upon Hector Mackintosh, cawand himself captain of the Clanchattan and others, his accomplices and partakers, and inward them to slachter, hership and fire ... taking their goods to himself for his labours.

In 1535 the King gave James a special charter, exempting him from the jurisdiction of all courts except the newly instituted Court of Session in Edinburgh, and in 1540 he ordered Patrick, Bishop of Moray, to grant to James Grant the lands of the barony of Strathspey that were not already broken into smaller landholdings, so that this land be set in feus. James Grant was also the Bailie to the Abbot of Kinloss, and in 1544 appointed Alexander Cumming of Altyre his Bailie Depute.

Castle Grant is reckoned to be haunted by the ghost of Lady Barbara Grant – said to have been a daughter of a sixteenth-century laird, and hence possibly the daughter of James of the Forays. According to the traditional tale, she fell in love with a lad from the nearby village, though her father regarded this lad as being of inferior rank. Her father had made arrangements for a marriage to someone he deemed more suitable, but Barbara disagreed. As a punishment he locked her up in the windowless closet of the uppermost bedroom of the old tower, thinking that a few days' imprisonment would bring her to his way of thinking, but it only made the girl's resolve grow stronger. He kept her locked up for a few weeks more, till at length she died. Her ghost is still sometimes seen in the 'Haunted Room', flitting to and fro. Sometimes she seems to stop halfway and wash her hands before continuing.

James Grant died in 1553. He was succeeded by his eldest son,

John, who at first was known as Iain Baold, or 'John the Gentle', in contrast to his father's fierceness. His second son, Archibald, was the progenitor of the Grants of Cullen and Monymusk, among other branches.

12   Gunn of Kilearnan
The Stolen Daughter

The Clan Gunn had their seat at Kilearnan, eight miles up Strath Ullie from Helmsdale in Sutherland. They claim descent from Gunni, son of Olave (or Olaf) the Black, King of Man and the Isles (d 1237), himself son of Sweyn Asleifsson, the 'Ultimate Viking', who was slain at Dublin in 1171. Gunni acquired his lands through marriage, but the clan was a warlike one – indeed it may even get its name from the Norse gunnr, which means 'war'. Its motto is aut pax aut bellum, 'either peace or war' – but war seems to have been the preferred option!

The Gunns had long feuded with a number of their neighbours in the north of Scotland. They were often at war with the Mackays, and they became involved in the arguments between the Sutherlands (whom they supported) and the Sinclairs. Sir Robert Gordon, compiler of *A Geneaological History of the Earldom of Sutherland*, written in the mid-seventeenth century, notes that 'the long, the many, the horrible encounters between these two trybes [the Gunns and Mackays], with the bloodshed and infinit spoils committed in every part of the diocy of Catteynes by them and their associats, are of so disordered and troublesome memorie'.

The Gunns' most hated enemy were the Keiths of Ackergill. The hatred seems to date back to the early fifteenth century. Lachlan Gunn of Braemore, a crofting clachan or township on the banks of the Berriedale Water in Caithness, had an only daughter, Helen, who was renowned in the district as the Beauty of Braemore. It was arranged that she would marry her cousin, Alexander Gunn, and the two readily agreed to this. However, Helen had another admirer who was willing to stop at nothing to gain her hand in marriage: Dugald Keith, a retainer of the Keiths of Ackergill Tower, which stood on a rock overlooking Sinclair's Bay. (Some accounts claim Dugald, or Dougal, was actually the Chief of the Keiths, but this is uncertain).

Keith had proposed to her a number of times before, but each time he was spurned, for she had promised her love to another. Dugald tried once more, only to be told that she was spoken for, and that the wedding day was planned. He panicked and decided that he must act fast to make the beautiful Helen his wife. He was so desperate that he was willing to kidnap her, and hoped that, when she saw just how deeply in love with her he was, she would fall for his charms. On the morning of the proposed wedding, Dugald gathered a body of Keiths and led them south to Braemore. They surrounded the old house, and Dugald called out to the Gunns within. Unprepared for an attack, and busily getting ready for the day's celebrations, they were quickly overwhelmed and many of them died in the melee – among them Alexander, the bridegroom.

The fair Helen was tied to the back of a horse and taken back the long moorland miles to Ackergill. She still refused to become Dugald Keith's bride, despite his pleadings, so he had her locked up in one of the castle's topmost turrets, from where, it was said, she would spend much of her time looking out of a window towards Braemore, awaiting the arrival of the Gunns. This angered Dugald so much that he ordered the estate mason to block up the window. After a time, when her lover had not turned up to save her, Helen threw herself from the remaining turret window and died when she hit a large boulder in the courtyard below. This stone is still pointed out in the castle courtyard, and the spirit of the Beauty of Braemore is said to haunt the tower as a Green Lady.

Lachlan Gunn and his family had not forgotten the fair Helen, however. They made a number of attacks on Keith lands, but each time they were repelled. One battle took place in 1426, at Harpsdale, eight miles from Thurso, the place name and its memory survives in the place name of the Bloody Moss, beside the River Thurso. The encounter was bloody indeed, and there were numerous casualties, but the outcome was indecisive. Another battle took place in 1438 at Tannach Moor, four miles from Wick, where the Gunns were defeated by the Keiths and Mackays. And at Dirlot, further up the Thurso River from Harpsdale, they suffered another defeat.

The feud between the Gunns and Keiths continued for 40 years. In 1464 George Gunn was chief of the clan, residing at Clyth Castle (long since crumbled into the sea but magnificently sited nine miles south-west of Wick on Halberry Head, the neck of which is only 150 feet wide). He was Coroner of Caithness – the office of coroner, or crowner, was created in the mid-fourteenth century by the Scots kings, and coroners were responsible for keeping the peace in their own areas, rather like sheriffs, and also seem to have been responsible for investigating murders, raising troops for the king's service, and arresting those who broke the peace.

'Crowner' George Gunn felt that a coroner should not be embroiled in a feud, so he decided to settle the quarrel between the two families once and for all. He met with the chieftain of the Keiths of Ackergill and they agreed a method of settling the dispute. Each clan should send twelve horses bearing soldiers to an appointed spot, and the result of the fight between them would settle the matter forever.

George led eleven other mounted Gunn soldiers along the road to the rendezvous: the Chapel of St Tears, or St Tayr, that once stood between Noss Head and Ackergill. They were confident of the outcome, for the soldiers chosen were the strongest in the country and renowned for their agility and skill. They soon spotted the Keiths approaching from the opposite direction and, after counting the twelve horses in the distance, just to check that there was no cheating, were satisfied that the agreed terms had been fulfilled. When the horses came closer, though, and the Gunns were able to see more clearly, they realised that each of the twelve horses had two men mounted on it.

The Keiths galloped towards the Gunns, and the fight ensued. The outnumbered Gunns fought valiantly but in vain and were all cut to pieces by the swords of the Keiths, (some accounts state that two Gunns survived the battle and were found wounded the following morning by men of their clan.) George Gunn fell to the ground, dead, and was stripped of his armour, and the Ackergill chieftain stole his coroner's badge, the large silver brooch which held his plaid together. Delighted with their victory, and pleased to have gained the large brooch of the Coroner, from which George Gunn had been known as Am Bràisteach Mór ('the big brooch-wearer'), the Keiths returned to Ackergill.

It is related by some that the Crowner's five sons, who had watched the fight from a distance, decided to trail the Keiths as they made their way back home; the youngest, Eanruig, or Henry, suggested trying to win back their father's badge and sword. They followed the Keiths to Dalraid Castle, where they were celebrating their victory, and Eanruig managed to climb up the stone masonry of the fortress and look at the Keiths rejoicing in the great hall. He took his bow and shot an arrow through the narrow slit, piercing the chieftain's heart. As the crowd looked in shock at their murdered leader they heard the young lad yell, 'The compliments of the Gunns to Keith.'

The feud was not over yet, however. A grandson of George Gunn by the name of William MacKames (a name which is a sept of the Clan Gunn) gathered together ten men and pursued George Keith's son, also George. As Keith passed Drummoy in Sutherland, en route to Caithness, they attacked him, killing both him and his son, as well as ten retainers. Some old Gaelic verses commemorate this event.

Having lost their chief and many of their best soldiers, the Gunns lost their authority in the district, and by 1594 were listed as one of the 'broken clans' of the north of Scotland. They remained chiefless thereafter, and no one today is recognised as head of the family.

The feud between the Gunns and the Keiths officially came to an end on 28 July 1978. On that day the Earl of Kintore, Chief of the Clan Keith, and Ian Gunn, Commander of Clan Gunn (in the absence of a recognised chief) met at the site of the Chapel of St Tears. During a short ceremony, both leaders signed a peace treaty in front of many clansmen who were attending the gathering of Clan Gunn.

13   Lamont of that Ilk
The Evil Massacre

On the Castle Hill in the Argyllshire town of Dunoon, in Tom a' Mhoid Road, is a roughly-hewn memorial boulder, inscribed with a Celtic cross. Erected by the Clan Lamont Society in 1906, it commemorates a great massacre of the clan Lamont which occurred in 1646.

At the beginning of the seventeenth century the head of the Lamonts was Sir James Lamont of that Ilk, 14th Chief of the clan and descendant of Laumun, who founded the tribe in the thirteenth century. James married a daughter of Sir Colin Campbell of Ardkinglas and succeeded his father in 1635. He was regarded as a good chief, representing Argyll in Parliament in 1634, as his father had done before him, and he established a school on the lands of Toward in 1643. He was a royalist, and joined MacLeod of Dunvegan, MacDonald of Sleat, Stuart of Bute, Maclean of Duart, Stewart of Ardgowan, and other notables in planning the restoration of the liturgy in the Scottish church, and reclaiming church lands which many nobles had acquired. However, the Calvinist chief of the Campbells, who held considerable sway in Argyll, discovered this, and warned Lamont to back off, threatening him with various reprisals.

King Charles I regarded Sir James as a friend, and during the Civil War sent him a commission to deal with some of the rebels in his part of the country, which of course included Argyll. At first Lamont was scared to use his royal commission and decided it would be prudent to side with Argyll. He followed him in battle at Inverlochy on 2 February 1645, but did so half-heartedly and was easily taken prisoner. The Marquis of Montrose, realising that he was really a supporter of the king, released him from jail and gave him a second royal commission.

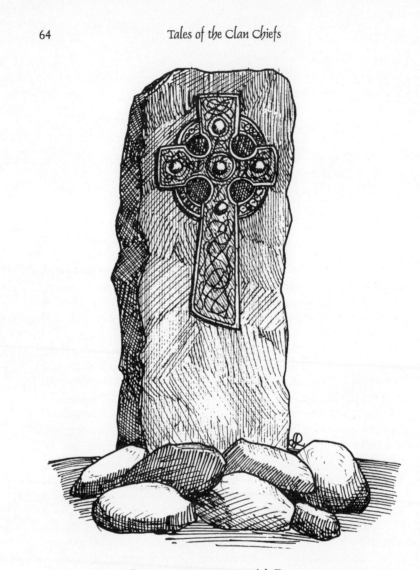

Lamont massacre memorial, Dunoon

The commission allowed him to attack the Campbell rebels, and he was delighted to get the chance to perhaps regain some of the old Lamont homelands. He was joined by a party of MacDonalds and MacDonells, also long-standing enemies of the Campbells, and harried much of Argyll – perhaps with rather too much zeal, for they were described by the Covenanters as 'a most cruel, horrid, and bloody band'. The Lamonts and MacDonalds then split up, and the

Lamonts continued to attack homes and settlements in the county, among them the Castle of Ardkinglas even though it was the home of the chief's brother-in-law. The journey home led close to Strachur, where a number of homeless Campbells had been given shelter, and in revenge for this the Lamonts killed 33 residents and looted and destroyed many of their homes. Before they reached Glen Branter word had reached the inhabitants, who fled their homes; only one old and disabled man was left behind, and it is recorded that he was stripped of his clothes and left outside to die of exposure.

The Lamonts then attacked the castle of Kilmun on the shores of the Holy Loch. The keeper of the castle, a Campbell to whom Sir James Lamont had once been tutor, agreed to surrender the tower with the promise of quarter. As soon as the Lamonts had taken the occupants prisoner, however, they changed their tune and decided to put them to death. They were bound, made to walk about three miles along the side of the loch and then massacred, apart from one person who was suffering badly 'in the hot fever' – even he did not avoid death, for he was killed in the village kirk.

With the death of the Marquis of Montrose the fortunes of the Campbells improved, and they were not long in seeking retribution. In 1646 Campbell of Ardkinglas struck across Cowal at Toward Castle, seat of the Lamont chief. Sir James was at home and, when he saw the large party of Campbells making their way to his castle, realised that it was futile to try and fight them. From the battlements he called to Ardkinglas, and it was agreed that the two should parley. Lamont and Ardkinglas discussed the situation for a while, and Lamont was able to persuade the attacker to let him and his follow-ers go in return for the castle and lands. A document was written up to this effect, and Campbell signed his name at the foot.

> It is agreed that the said Sir James Lamont shall overgive his house at Toward and shall have libertie to goe himself, his brethren, souldiers, wives and children, towards Sir Alexander MacDonnald or anie of his quarters, who for that effect shall have a safe conduct, and boates sent along, who shall deliver them without anie harm of any person to bee done to them, under the said James's command, without prejudice to such women as intend to go to the east side of the Isle of Boote to be safely conducted there with boats.

Sir James then went with the Campbells to negotiate with the Lamonts at Ascog Castle, which stood beside a loch of the same name, a few miles from Tighnabruaich. This was another of Sir James's properties but was lived in by some of his relatives, and they too surrendered their stronghold. The treaty made no mention of protecting the Lamont castles, and it was not long before both towers were looted and burnt. Toward Castle was almost totally destroyed, and remains a ruin to this day, as does Ascog. From the Lamont fields the Campbells lifted over 3,000 cattle which they drove back to Argyll.

The Campbells failed to adhere to the written bond, however, for fresh in their memories was the incident at Kilmun, in which the Lamonts had failed to keep their word. Most of the Lamont clansmen, women and children were transported to Dunoon Castle where they were kept imprisoned for eight days. The rest were taken to the kirkyard where they were massacred – among them the unfortunate Provost of Rothesay, unlucky enough to have been visiting his relatives at Toward when the Campbells attacked. An old account relates what happened:

> After plundering and robbing all that was within and about the said house, most barbarously, inhumanly, and cruelly murdered several, young and old, yea, sucking children, some of them not one month old, and that the said persons, defendants, or one or others of them, contrary to the foresaid capitulations, our laws, and acts of Parliament, upon the – day of June 1646, most traiterously and perfidiously did carry the whole people who were in the said houses of Escog and Towart in boats to the village of Dunoone, and there most cruelly, traiterously, and perfidiously, murthered, without assyse or order of law, by shotts, by durks, by cutting their throats, as they doe with beasts, above ane hundreth, and lastly they cause hang upon one tree near the number of thirty-six persons, most of them being SPECIAL GENTLEMEN of the name Lamont, and vassals to the said Sir James, and before they were half hanged they cutt them downe and threw them in by dozens in pitts prepared for the same; and many of them striveing to ryse upon their feet were violently holden downe untill that by throwing the earth in great quantity upon them they were stifled to death.

According to the *New Statistical Account*, to show His displeasure at such cruelty, 'the Lord struck the said [ash] tree immediately thereafter'. It remained standing but lifeless for two years before being cut down, after which the remaining roots seeped a red substance like blood. This ran in 'several streams' for many years until those responsible for the massacre had the roots dug from the ground and the area covered with fresh soil.

Two Lamonts were taken from Dunoon to Inveraray, where they faced a mock trial in front of the Campbell judge and jury. Not surprisingly, they were found guilty of their crimes and hanged. Sir James Lamont, however, was not executed at Dunoon with his clansmen. He was taken back north into Argyll and held prisoner in the dungeon pit at Dunstaffnage Castle, north of Oban. He was later moved to the island castle of Inchconnell, in Loch Awe, another Campbell stronghold. He was kept locked up for five long years. It is said that he was not allowed to change his clothes, and that he died around 1651 in the very same garments he had been wearing when Castle Toward was attacked.

One of the few Lamonts allowed to live after the attack on Castle Toward was Sir James' sister, Lady Isobel. She kept the promissory note from the Campbells which offered safe conduct, and, to avoid it being stolen, folded it into a long, narrow strip which she braided through her hair. There it remained until she was in complete safety. After Charles II regained the throne she produced the letter, revealing the sufferings of the Lamonts and their treatment at the hand of the Campbells. The evidence was sufficient to allow the Lamonts to claim compensation.

14 MacAlister of Loup
The Midnight Burning

The MacAlisters of the Loup claim descent from the great Clan Donald. Alasdair Mor was a son of Donald of Islay, Lord of the Isles, who was himself the grandson of Somerled, the half-Viking, half-Scots King of the Hebrides and Argyll. The lineage grew in number, until in 1493 it was regarded as a separate clan. Alasdair Mor's family had settled at a place known as The Loup (or Lowb) in Kintyre, on the south side of West Loch Tarbert, and in 1481 Charles MacAlister was appointed Steward of Knapdale and Constable of the royal castle of Tarbert (with this he received a grant of lands nearby). Not all the MacAlister chiefs were so loyal to the crown; in the late sixteenth and early seventeenth centuries a number of them were involved in clan feuds, and one of them was denounced as a rebel.

Godfrey MacAlister became the fifth Chief of his clan while still a youth, when his father Alasdair (or Alexander) died in 1587. Thereafter he was brought up with a relative who also acted as his 'Tutor', as was the custom at the time. 'Gorrie' as he was better known, became acquainted with the young daughter of a neighbouring laird of considerable wealth and possessions, and they were often seen together, exchanging gifts and romancing. Godfrey's tutor was displeased at this love match and did all in his power to try and separate the pair (it was reckoned that he wanted the young woman as a bride for one of his own sons). It seems that the tutor succeeded in causing a rift between the young lovers, and they fell out. However, Godfrey later discovered that this had been set up by his guardian and, not unnaturally, was angered. Having reached adulthood, he was a fit man, very able to seek his revenge, and when the tutor became aware that Gorrie had discovered his ploy he feared for his life, leaving Kintyre and living for a time in a distant part of the country. Gorrie meanwhile bided his time and awaited his return.

The tutor came back to Kintyre in 1598, and Gorrie was not long in searching him out. The two met, and a struggle ensued in which young MacAlister killed the tutor. The tutor's sons, who had been involved in their father's plot against the chief, took fright and fled for protection to Askomill, on the north shore of Campbeltown Loch, the town-house of Angus MacDonald of Dunyveg.

Angus had been Chief of the Clan Iain Mhor, one of the septs of MacDonald, since 1566 but proved a rather inept chieftain. James VI had previously issued a warrant for his arrest, for some unknown crime, and through mismanagement and incompetence he had lost most of the clan lands. Angus's son, Sir James MacDonald of Knockrinsay in Islay, who had fallen out with his father over this incompetence and was keen to wreak some form of vengeance against him, thus welcomed Gorrie MacAlister's suggestion that the two of them should gather their supporters, MacDonalds and MacAlisters, and attack Askomill.

Gorrie and Sir James headed towards Askomill under the cover of darkness. With them were Sir James's younger brother Angus (executed in 1615 for his part in the Lord of the Isles' uprising), the laird of Largie Castle, and a force of 300 clansmen described as 'the haill tennentis of Kintyre'. According to a contemporary account they were armed with 'hagbuittis, pistolletis, axes, bowes, targeis, two handit swordis and uther invasive wapines'. Only a slight moon and the stars lit their way, but Sir James knew the countryside well, having crossed it many times at all hours of the day and night. When they reached Askomill, Gorrie banged at the door and called out to those inside, 'Come out and surrender, or else we will attack'. The occupants refused to open the door, and yelled from an upper window that they would not capitulate. 'Then we will smoke you out,' hollered Sir James.

The men gathered together bracken and hay from close by, and a taper was lit and offered up to the bonfire, which was soon billowing smoke. Sparks flew into the black sky, and a few landed on the thatched roof, setting it alight. When the house caught fire quicker than expected, some of the men tried to persuade Sir James that they should now extinguish it, for his father and mother were also in the house. He steadfastly refused, saying, 'They will come out of the house themselves when they are ready'. The fire burned on, so fiercely that it seemed that no one could still be alive inside the building.

Suddenly the front door burst open, and a few members of the household ran out. Sir James had laid tree branches across the threshold to trip anyone leaving, and Angus MacDonald stumbled over them and slumped to the ground, choking violently from the smoke and with many severe burn marks on his clothes and body. The rest of the household were similarly affected.

Angus alone was taken prisoner, being tied at the wrists and ankles. He was tortured by the clansmen under Sir James and taken to John MacKay's castle at Smerby, a few miles to the north, where he was held prisoner. He was later moved to Saddell Castle, where he was held in the vaults for a further two nights before Sir James took him by boat to Dumbarton and handed him over to the authorities at the castle garrison.

The government reckoned that Sir James's use of force in arresting his father had been rather too severe, and that his actions had bordered on the criminal. An order from the Privy Council in Edinburgh was sent to Dumbarton Castle, allowing Angus to go free, so long as he promised to keep the peace thereafter. It was felt that his treatment at the hands of his son was sufficient punishment for his crimes.

After this incident Gorrie MacAlister and Sir James MacDonald had to make themselves scarce for a while. They came to prominence again later the same year, when on 5 August they fought at the Battle of Traigh Ghruineart on the island of Islay. This was a conflict between the MacDonalds and the MacLeans. The latter, who had been trying to claim the lands of the Rinns of Islay, were heavily defeated and their chief slain. Thereafter Gorrie seems to have settled, for in September 1605, when Sir David Murray, Lord Scone, was sent to Kintyre to get the signatures of the principal chiefs as surety for their adherence to the King and for payment of all taxes and dues, he was one of the few who turned up. Godfrey MacAlister died not long after this, and was taken to the island of Iona for burial, the last resting place of his ancestors.

Sir James MacDonald's life had a different ending. He was condemned as a traitor in 1609. Old Angus managed to capture him, and he was passed over to Campbell of Auchinbreck, who passed him on to the Earl of Argyll. Sir James was then sent to stand before the Privy Council in Perth who charged him with treason and fire-raising. He was sentenced to death, but escaped from Edinburgh Castle in 1615 and headed back to Islay where he was able to reclaim some of his lands. However, the authorities pursued him, and he was forced to emigrate to Spain. Though he received a pardon in 1620, he was forbidden to return to Scotland.

15 MacDonald of Clanranald
Black Donald the Cruel

One of the major branches of Clan Donald is Clanranald, descended from Ranald MacDonald, the son of John MacDonald, first Lord of the Isles, who lived at the end of the fourteenth century. The principal seat of the clan for many years was Castle Tioram, which stands on a rocky islet in tidal Loch Moidart. The castle wall has five irregular sides, following the shape of the rock, and the seaward wall has no window as an added protection against attack from ships. Today a ruin, the castle is accessible from the mainland when the tide is low, hence its name, Eilean Tioram, Gaelic for 'dry island'.

One of the most infamous of all clan chiefs was Donald MacDonald, 13th Chief of Clanranald. He was born sometime around 1625, and succeeded his father John in 1670. Both father and son joined Montrose's army during the Civil War. Donald MacDonald developed into an evil character, with a weird love of shooting. He was wont to stand on the battlements of Castle Tioram and fire at anything that moved. Many a seagull was shot from the sky, basking seals were unsafe on the rocks around the fortress, and, since the shore was within range of the castle, MacDonald would often aim at animals walking along the wooded hillside of Cruach nam Meann. For some unknown reason, his Spanish long gun was known by everyone as 'the cuckoo', and its owner was dubbed Domhnall Dubh na Cuthaige, or 'black Donald of the Cuckoo'.

One day a man was wandering along the pathway that led along the shore. MacDonald was on the battlements at the time, shooting at seabirds, when he spotted the man among the trees. The chief looked at him for a while, but did not recognise him, so lifted his gun and took aim. The shot rang out over the loch, and MacDonald watched the distant man stumble and fall to the ground – some say

A Highlander

that he fell into a well or spring. The chief's retainers left the castle island to see who the man was, and they were shocked to discover that he was a notable local figure and one of the principal members of their clan known as the Lad of the Wet Feet. He gained this name from his role of walking in front of the chief to check that the ground was not boggy and, if it was, to redirect his chief's steps.

One day Donald MacDonald found some of his money was missing. His suspicions fell upon three members of his household, his own personal ghillie and two servants, one male, the other female. The three were summoned to the castle's great hall where the chief questioned them about the missing money, but all three denied any knowledge of it. MacDonald's suspicions remained, however, for he thought that their answers had been unsatisfactory, and he had the two men dragged out of the castle to the local dule, or hanging tree, and strung up. The maidservant was not hanged; she was taken by boat to one of the tidal rocks near the mouth of Loch Moidart, tied by her long hair to a stake hammered into the ground and was left to drown as the tide came in. The rock was known thereafter as the 'rock of James's daughter'. It is said that during road-building operations in the late nineteenth century workmen found the hidden money beneath a boulder adjacent to the now demolished Dorlin House.

These three servants were not the only members of Clanranald's household to suffer execution at their master's hands. The cook who worked in the castle kitchen was fond of snuff, and was not averse to taking some from the chief's special snuff-box. On one occasion she was caught by the chief, who had her taken to the castle prison. He decided that she was to be hanged on the dule-tree, and some of his men walked her to the Hanging Hill where the tree grew. Somehow (no one knows how) the cook had managed to steal the snuff-box from the castle, and as they made their way to the place of execution, the cook produced it from her person and defiantly took a large pinch of its contents; just as the chief realised it was his own special snuff-mull, the cook threw it far into the waters of the loch. The spot where she was hanged has been known as Tom na Caillich, or 'the old wife's mound', ever since.

Another, unidentified, person was executed by Black Donald inside the castle. Evidence of the death survived for many years after the event, for in one of the castle dungeons there was a blood-spattered floor which could not be cleaned: the stain stubbornly remained, no matter how many times it was scraped off or washed.

Donald MacDonald's first wife was Janet MacDonald of Sleat, but the marriage appears to have been childless. He then married his first cousin, Marion MacLeod, by whom he had three daughters and a son, Allan Ruaridh, who succeeded him and subsequently died at the battle of Sheriffmuir in 1715. There is a tradition that some chief had his wife imprisoned in Coroghon Castle on the island of Canna in 1666, and it is often said that this was Donald the Cruel and that his wife was in love with a MacNeil from Barra. The prison was not totally secure however, for the lady managed to escape one night by tying her blankets into a rope and scrambling down the castle walls. It is known that in 1680 Donald started divorce proceedings against her, citing desertion and adultery. It is also claimed that he found her in bed with a priest from Inverness.

One legend claims that MacDonald was haunted by a large dark-coloured toad. Everywhere he went, this creature seemed to appear, and it got on the chief's nerves. He sent for the local priest, but for some unknown reason failed to have the spirit exorcised – either he failed to turn up or else he was unsuccessful in getting rid of it. He also tried various other methods of disposing of it: he shot the toad a couple of times with 'the cuckoo', but this seems not to have worked, and he locked it up in the castle pit, but again it managed to escape and appear by the chief's side. One day the chief and his men were sailing out towards the island of Eigg, and the toad seemed to be following the boat. Well out into the Sound of Arisaig a storm blew up and threatened to sink the boat. The sailors, reckoning that the toad was the manifestation of some form of evil spirit, pleaded to the chief to lift it aboard, but Clanranald laughed at them and said he would rather ride out the storm in the hope that it would kill the toad. Wind shredded the boat's sails, and the waves lunged over the side, so the hull was filling with water and sinking was imminent. At this point the men told the chief that if he failed to bring the toad aboard they would drop their oars. Reluctantly the chief agreed, and once the black toad was safely on board the storm miraculously disappeared.

Donald MacDonald received a charter of the island of Canna from the Marquis of Argyll in 1672, and thereafter spent much of his time on the island, where he died in 1686. There are tales of mysterious happenings at the time of his death. As he lay in bed the members of his household were wakened by a loud noise, a constant piercing note which rang through their heads and caused them to cover their ears. Where the sound came from no one could discover, but it seemed to ring loudest nearest the chief. At one point the screech became so loud that the chief ran outdoors, where he thought it would be quieter. Members of the household ran after the chief, recognising that he was in a fit of madness and was likely to injure himself, and managed to drag him back indoors, but he struggled so much that they had to tie him to his bed. The sound continued for the rest of the night, but seemed to wane somewhat as time went on. As dawn arrived the cock crowed three times, and the chief died.

The supernatural happenings did not cease with the chief's death, however. A storm blew up which lashed at the island for seven weeks, preventing any boat from landing or departing. Only when the waves began to subside and the winds die down was the corpse of Donald Dubh able to be transported across the Minch to Howmore, on the island of South Uist, where he was buried.

An old story gives a reason for the storm. According to this, there was a priest on the island of Canna who wished to cross the Minch to the Uists. But apparently he had preached a sermon in which he harangued the chief for his treatment of his wife. Donald of the Cuckoo was therefore unwilling to let the holy man leave the island, and to prevent him doing so had a plank removed from the hull of every boat on the island. As a result the priest was stuck on Canna until one day a boat was passing close to the shore and the priest hollered across the waters to it. The captain heard his cries, and came into the bay and picked up the priest. Safely aboard, and gratified to find out that the boat was headed for Loch Eynort on South Uist, the priest faced the island and cursed the chief: 'I do not ask that your soul be tormented, but may your corpse be kept unburied here as long as you have kept me.'

16 MacDonell of Keppoch
The Well of the Heads

One of the most famous clan chiefs was Colonel Alastair Ranaldson MacDonell, 15th Chief of the MacDonells of Glengarry (1771–1828), who is said to have been the last Highland chief to live according to the ancient feudal customs of the Highlands. He was never seen without full Highland dress, complete with the three eagle feathers which denoted his chiefship, and when he travelled anywhere he was not to be seen without his 'tail' of servants. In 1812 Henry Raeburn painted a famous portrait depicting MacDonell standing proudly in red tartan hose, kilt with sporran, tartan plaid and Glengarry bonnet. MacDonell founded the Highland Society in 1815, to promote 'the dress, language, music and characteristics of our illustrious and ancient race in the Highlands and Isles of Scotland, with their genuine descendants wherever they may be'.

Glengarry at one time took part in a duel with the grandson of Flora MacDonald, the Jacobite heroine. Glengarry won, but he was taken to court, and it required the skill of his lawyer, Henry Erskine, to prevent his execution. MacDonell greeted King George IV when he visited Edinburgh in 1822, and he was a friend of Sir Walter Scott, who is said to have based the character of Fergus MacIvor of Glennaquoich in *Waverley* upon him. In January 1828 MacDonell was sailing up Loch Linnhe on the steamer *Stirling Castle* when the ship struck a rock in Inverscaddle Bay and foundered. He tried to jump to safety but slipped on the seaweed-covered rocks and sustained head injuries of which he died a few hours later. At his death MacDonell was deeply in debt – owing in excess of £80,000.

In 1812 MacDonell of Glengarry had erected a memorial on the shores of Loch Oich to commemorate an incident in the clan's history which took place in September 1663. The memorial, visible to motorists driving along the lochside on the A82, consists of a squat obelisk with a carved stone finial depicting seven heads, the hair of which is bound together to a dirk. The memorial stands by the Tobar nan Ceann, which translates as the 'well of the heads'. The inscriptions on the memorial, in English, Gaelic, Latin and French, have been described as 'pompous' and 'inaccurate' by many historians, for they date the incident to early in the sixteenth century.

Tobar nan Ceann

Donald Glas MacDonald of Keppoch, 11th Chief of that branch of Clan Donald, sent his two sons to Rome to be educated. When he died, around 1649, his sons were still abroad, and the estate was run by a tutor, Donald Glas's brother, Alasdair Buidhe. When the two sons returned to Lochaber the elder, Alasdair of Keppoch, became very unpopular, apparently for trying to foist foreign ideas on his clansmen. He nursed a grievance against a branch of the MacDonalds who had been settled for at least a century at Inverlair, five miles up Glen Spean from Keppoch Castle. He reckoned that he held superiority over their lands, but MacDonald of Inverlair had obtained a lease from the Earl of Huntly, whom the Crown regarded as the superior; the Inverlair family, known as the Siol Dughaill, or race of Dougal, even had some claim to the chiefship of Keppoch.

Alasdair of Keppoch travelled up the glen and attacked Inverlair, reiving their cattle, and leaving the family homeless. MacDonald of Inverlair thereupon sent a complaint to the Privy Council, and Alasdair of Keppoch lodged a counter-complaint. On the morning of 5 September 1663 a group of Inverlair supporters attacked Keppoch Castle, armed with dirks, swords and other weapons. They rampaged through the building, and when they discovered Alasdair and his brother Ranald a fight ensued. Outnumbered, the pair were soon slaughtered, and the Inverlair men returned home. It was said that there was no great grief for the loss of the two brothers, rather that a great sense of relief settled in the district (Alasdair Buidhe, the lads' uncle, was even suspected of having been involved in the murders, but there was never any proof).

One person was determined to avenge the murders, however, even though the father of the murderers was his sister's husband. This person was John MacDonald, better known as Iain Lom, the 'beardless bard' of Keppoch. As the chief's personal bard, he had been particularly close to the brothers. He rode to Invergarry Castle, the ruins of which still stand on the shore of Loch Oich, where he appeared before MacDonell of Glengarry. He pleaded for the chief to help him in seeking out the murderers, but he was turned down, for there were rumours that the deaths had been accidental. He then turned his attention to Sir James MacDonald of Sleat, whose seat was Armadale Castle on the island of Skye. It was he who had fostered the two Keppoch lads in their youth. Again, support was not forthcoming. Undeterred, however, Iain Lom returned to MacDonald of Sleat a number of times over a two-year period until he had persuaded the chief that something should be done. Sleat contacted the Privy Council and received from them a commission of fire and sword, which allowed him to take the matter into his own hands.

It is said that Iain Lom also approached a local rogue, known as Iain Odhar Campbell, who lived at Roybridge, to ask him to take part in the revenge. Iain Odhar was a noted mercenary, and was infamous for his exploits, for which he charged a fee. He had escaped the gallows a number of times, because the local people were frightened to stand against him. However, being a Campbell living in the heart of Clan Donald land, he turned Iain Lom down, saying, 'No, no. If I put my hands in your blood, you will put your hands in mine tomorrow.'

Iain Lom and fifty men who had been loaned by Sleat made their way up Glen Spean. The Sleat men were led by Archibald MacDonald of North Uist, another bard, known as An Ciaran Mabach, or 'the lisping swarthy man'. They arranged themselves around the old house of Inverlair, but found entry barred and the windows shuttered. Undeterred, they battered the door down, entered the building and set fire to straw on the ground floor. The smoke billowed up the staircase of the building, and the men upstairs realised that they would have to try and escape from the house and face those below, or else remain where they were and die of asphyxiation. They decided to take their chances and headed for the door. As the Inverlair men staggered from their house, their eyes streaming from the smoke, the attackers ran their swords through them. Seven were killed in total; their heads were severed, and the corpses were buried in a low mound to the east of the house. The heads, however, were tied together by the hair of their beards and roped to the back of Iain Lom's horse. He set off north to Invergarry Castle. At a natural spring on the shores of Loch Oich he stopped to wash them at a well that was an ancient Celtic site that had some association with the skull, and may already have been known as Tobar nan Ceann.

At Invergarry Iain Lom was ushered into the great hall, where he placed the seven heads before MacDonell. He told the chief that he, Iain Lom, knew his duty, and he chastised the chief for failing to act. He then went to Skye with the heads and presented them to MacDonald of Sleat as proof that justice had been achieved. Word that the murders had been avenged was sent to the Privy Council, which responded by thanking Iain Lom for 'the good service done to his majesty'.

To commemorate his part in the feud the bard of Keppoch composed a lament entitled Mort na Ceapaich (Death of Keppoch) which details the events. He had been created poet laureate in Scotland by Charles II at the time of the Restoration and was awarded a pension. Iain Lom died in 1710 at the age of 86 and was buried in the old kirkyard of Cille a' Choireal, in Glen Spean, where a memorial commemorates him. Keppoch Castle is said to have been pulled down by the clansmen after the murders within its walls, for they did not wish to be reminded of the horror which had happened there. The present Keppoch House was erected around 1760 by the 18th Chief.

In 1818 a general practitioner from Fort William, Dr Smith, and a few of his friends decided to investigate the green mound at Inverlair. They opened a trench in the tumulus and disinterred seven headless skeletons.

17 MacDougall of Lorn
The Brooch of Lorn

In the thirteenth century the MacDougalls were a very prominent clan. They had a number of notable castles – among them Dunstaffnage, Dunollie, Carn na Burgh Mor, Dunconnel and Gylen – and to service them, and to keep the law of the isles, they had a fleet of birlinns, or galleys. The chief of the MacDougalls at this time was Alexander, or Alasdair, son of 'King' Ewin of Argyll. Ewin had to decide whether his loyalties lay with the King of Norway or with the King of Scotland; he chose the latter, and refused to support King Haco at the Battle of Largs in 1263. Alexander was appointed the first Sheriff of Argyll when that former kingdom was converted into a Scottish shire in 1292.

Alexander was married to the third daughter of the Red Comyn, whom Robert the Bruce killed in the church at Dumfries at the start of his campaign for the crown of Scotland. As a result he became a sworn enemy of the Bruce. The two of them met in a skirmish at the Battle of Dalrigh (which means 'field of the king'), which took place in Strathfillan, near Tyndrum in Argyll, on 11 August 1306, shortly after Bruce had been defeated by the English under the Earl of Pembroke at Methven. The Bruce had only 300 followers, whereas MacDougall had a thousand fighting clansmen at his back – many of them MacNabs, a clan that had supported John Balliol's claim to the crown. The King was forced to make a hasty retreat from Dalrigh and is said to have thrown his claymore into Lochan nan Arm, the lochan of the weapon.

A number of MacDougalls pursued the King, who found himself surrounded by three stout clansmen. The first made a grasp for the bridle of his horse, but was unsuccessful in unseating him and Bruce managed to cut off his arm. The second grabbed hold of his stirrup, but again Bruce managed to fend him off. The third lunged at the King from his own horse, grabbing him round the throat from behind. The Bruce managed to throw him over his shoulders and killed him. However, the third MacDougall had grasped Bruce's clasp or brooch and wrenched it from his plaid, and it was found in the dead man's hand when his friends came to collect the corpses.

The Bruce made his escape, but he gathered together a new force, which he led north to Argyll in August 1308, with the intention of subduing the MacDougalls. Word of the King's advance reached the MacDougalls, who arranged themselves across the narrow Pass of Brander at the north end of Loch Awe. However, Bruce's spies spotted them in the distance, so he sent a small party of soldiers to follow a circuitous route and attack the MacDougalls from the rear. Dropping from the slopes of Cruachan Beann, this party engaged the MacDougalls. The sons of Lorn thought the conflict would be an easy one, for the numbers were fewer than they had expected. Although the fighting was fierce, the MacDougalls scented a quick and decisive victory. But then the greater portion of the royal forces attacked from the opposite side. Surprised, the MacDougalls did the best they could, but they were surrounded by a greater force and realised that they had little chance. Most of them began to flee for their lives, scrambling up the steep slopes of the pass to try and avoid their pursuers. Alexander MacDougall, the chief of the clan, made his way onto a small vessel anchored in the salt-water Loch Etive. With a band of trusted men around him, he made his way down through the treacherous Falls of Lora to the Firth of Lorne. The boat was drawn up in the Bay of Dunstaffnage, and the chief took refuge in the castle which had been built by his father.

Robert the Bruce spent some time laying waste the lands of Lorn before he turned his attentions on the castle, which stands on a great boss of rock protected by a massive curtain wall. The MacDougalls held out for some time but eventually surrendered to the king, and the chief was allowed to swear homage to Bruce, instead of losing his life. His son John, however, refused to do this, and made his escape to England.

The Bruce was in the habit of destroying the castles he captured, but in the case of Dunstaffnage he decided to keep it complete and had it garrisoned in his name. In 1321 he appointed Arthur Campbell as Constable of the castle, and the Campbell family have held that office ever since, although the building is now in the care of Historic Scotland.

Alexander MacDougall died around 1310 and was probably buried at Ardchattan Priory, which had been founded in 1230 by his grandfather Duncan MacDougall. His successor, John MacDougall, fifth Chief of the clan, gave his support to Edward II of England and was appointed commander of the English fleet. Shortly after the English defeat at Bannockburn in 1314 he led the ships north to the Western Isles. Bruce pursued them, but he sailed across the Firth of Clyde and up Loch Fyne to Tarbert, where his men hauled the ships across the narrow isthmus, using planks of wood as slides and tree-trunks as rollers. (There was a long-standing tradition amongst the islanders that their lands would never be conquered unless the invader crossed this place; the last time this had happened had been when the Vikings portaged a long-ship across the isthmus and claimed the islands and Kintyre for the king of Norway.) Bruce's navy defeated John MacDougall's English force, and the chief's eldest son, Eoin Bacach or 'Lame John', was captured. He was taken south to Dumbarton Castle, where he was held prisoner for a time; in 1316 he was recorded as being held prisoner in Lochleven Castle, where he died.

Alexander's great-grandson, John, the son of Lame John, brought the MacDougall clan fully back into royal favour when he married Joanna, niece of King David II; in 1344 they were regranted the ancient clan lands. However they died without any male issue. A daughter married John Stewart, taking Lorn into that family, and the chiefship of MacDougall then passed to the Dunollie branch.

The Brooch of Lorn, as Bruce's brooch became known, has been passed down in the MacDougall family since 1306. At its centre is a large crystal of unusual colour (it has been described as resembling the glow from a peat fire) and around this is a circle of pearls. The centre of the brooch unscrews and formerly held a tiny fragment of bone – probably a relic of an early saint.

In 1647, during the Civil War, the brooch was in Gylen Castle for safe-keeping when it was attacked by a group of soldiers from General David Leslie's army. John MacDougall, the 19th Chief of the clan, and other members of his household refused General Leslie's demand for surrender, but it is thought that Leslie encamped outside the small courtyard, preventing the occupants of the tower from obtaining access to fresh water (the well was outside, on the promontory). After some time, the occupants surrendered, where-upon the castle was set on fire and most of its occupants massacred. According to an old Act of the Scots Parliament:

The Marquis of Argyle ... had caused burn Johne MacDowgall, his house of Gyland in the Yle of Kerrera, having threatened those that were therin with hanging to death if they did not burne the same. The said house was accordingly at his command brunt, and thereafter being forced to make capitulation with David Leslie and Colonel Holbourne, the leaders of the forces of the Marquis of Argyle, for the house of Dunollie ... And at last for the saifing of the wyves and children of those who wer murthered at Donnaverty and Kerrera being then all destitute of subsistance, and the said Johne MacDougall of Dunollie deducted to great miserie ... was forced to give over and quyte to the Marquis his heritable Bawllierie of Lorn.

During the raid the Brooch of Lorn was found and stolen by one of Leslie's officers, Campbell of Inverawe, and the MacDougalls thereafter assumed it to be lost. It was held in secret by the Campbells for almost two centuries, but in 1826 General Sir Duncan Campbell of Lochnell inherited the brooch and arranged for its return to the chief of the MacDougalls. At the time Patrick MacDougall, 24th Chief, was ill (he died within a few months), so his son, John, went to receive the brooch at a public ceremony at Inveraray Castle. It has remained the property of the MacDougall chiefs ever since, and today is kept at Dunollie House, home of the present MacDougall of MacDougall, the 31st Chief, which stands close to the ruins of the ancestral castle of Dunollie.

18   MacFarlane of Arrochar
MacFarlane's Lantern

In the Lowlands of Scotland the full moon was known as 'MacFarlane's lantern': an allusion to the clan's habit of using the moon to light its way on night-time cattle raids. (The clan had a pipe tune known as 'Thogail nam bò', which translates as 'lifting the cattle'). The MacFarlane home country was the mountainous lands around Arrochar and Loch Sloy, to the west of the northern end of Loch Lomond; 'Loch Sloigh' was in fact the old battle-cry of the clan, and on the shores of the loch is a hollow in the ground known as Sabhal MhicPhàrlain, or 'MacFarlane's Barn', a secret place where they could hide the stolen cattle. The ancient clan seats were at Inveruglas Castle (whose ruins stand on an islet in Loch Lomond), the castle on Eilean a' Bhuth (also in the midst of the loch), Tarbet and Arrochar. These places were well within striking distance of the rich Lennox farmlands, where many a herd of cattle was lost during the night.

The MacFarlanes were a wild lot in their day, and most of their feuds were as a result of cattle-reiving. One of their earliest campaigns, though, was to claim the Earldom of Lennox, to which their fifth chief, Malcolm MacFarlane, was male heir on the death of Donald, sixth Earl of Lennox in 1373. The effort failed, the title was granted to the Stewarts, and much acrimony between the families resulted. This was only settled in the fifteenth century, when the tenth Chief, Andrew MacFarlane, married a daughter of Sir John Stewart, Earl of Lennox, and their lands around Arrochar were confirmed to them. Thereafter, the MacFarlanes could dedicate their time to cattle-rustling.

They seem to have fought with every one of their neighbours, and in 1587 an Act of the Estates declared that the chief was responsible for the good behaviour of his clan. In 1594 the MacFarlanes were noted as being in the habit of committing robbery, theft and oppression, and a second Act describes the 'MacFerlanis of Arroquhar' as one of the 'clannis that hes capitanes, cheiffis and chiftanes quhome on thay depend, oft tymes aganis the willis of thair landlordis'. Donnachaidh Dubh, or Black Duncan, MacFarlane was responsible for burning a band of Atholl men whom he and a group of his clansmen discovered taking shelter in a wooden hut near Loch Sloy. Black Duncan's men surrounded the hut and managed to tie the door shut without those inside knowing what was happening; they set the building alight and burned the sleeping Atholl men alive.

One feud was between the MacFarlanes and the MacGregors, another clan noted for its cattle-lifting. On one occasion the MacFarlanes used hounds to help them hunt some MacGregor clansmen, and it is said that these dogs wore coats of chainmail to protect them against the enemy's arrows. There was also a long-standing feud with the Buchanans, whose lands were on the opposite bank of Loch Lomond. In January 1527 George and Robert 'Buchquhannane' were indicted 'for the treasonabell raising of fyre in the lands of Arrouchquir pertenying to MacFarlane', and it seems that a Buchanan killed a MacFarlane in the early seventeenth century; as retribution one of the Buchanans was captured and taken to MacFarlane country, where he endured a full day's torture before eventually being put to death.

Andrew MacFarlane, 14th Chief, had distinguished himself at the Battle of Langside in 1568, where he fought against Mary Queen of Scots, and the clan was responsible for capturing three of the Queen's banners. In 1592 he quarrelled with Sir Humphrey Colquhoun of Luss – his neighbour directly to the south and his mother's great nephew. Sir Humphrey had been having an affair with Andrew's wife, Agnes, and as a result MacFarlane and some of his clansmen murdered Colquhoun at the latter's castle of Bannachra, as detailed in Chapter 5.

At the beginning of the seventeenth century the chief of the clan was Andrew's son, John MacFarlane – it was probably he who had a memorial tablet erected in Luss kirkyard which noted that 'This is the place of burial appointed for the Lairds of Arrocwhar, 1612'. In 1610 John MacFarlane and two associates murdered a John Stewart in what was described as 'a maist barbarous manner'. A warrant was issued for the arrest as 'common thieves and murderers', and they were subsequently captured by Alexander Colquhoun of Luss, who transferred them into the custody of the garrison at Dumbarton Castle, from where they were taken under guard to the tolbooth of Edinburgh.

John MacFarlane was married four times, and each of his wives seems to have belonged to a family that his clan had feuded with over the years. His first wife was Susanna Buchanan, daughter of Sir George Buchanan of that Ilk, chief of the clan, but they had no issue. By his second wife, Helen – who was the daughter of Francis Stewart, Earl of Bothwell – he had his eldest son and heir, Walter. His third wife was Elizabeth Campbell, daughter of the Earl of Argyll, and the fourth was Margaret, daughter of James Murray of Struan. The first of these marriages does at least seem to have borne diplomatic fruit. In July 1624 the Privy Council called the chiefs of the MacFarlanes and the Buchanans to a special meeting at which the feud between them was to be settled by peaceful means. A jury of Highland lairds was assembled to oversee the decision, and John MacFarlane and his eldest son and heir, Walter, agreed to submit the quarrel to the council's judgement, as well as 'taking the burden on them for the whole clan'. A good number of the clan were tried and convicted of robbery and other crimes, many more were pardoned of their misdemeanours, whilst others were transported to the wild uplands of Aberdeen and Banff, where they were resettled. No further reference to a feud between the two clans is noted.

Thereafter, the clan was divided and many of its members were moved to live in different parts of Scotland. Like the MacGregors, the clan was proscribed in 1624, so that its members had to adopt other surnames, such as Greisock, MacCaudy, MacInnes, MacJames and Stewart. A number became MacAllans, or Allans, and this family claims descent from Allan MacFarlane, a younger son of the clan chief, who settled in the Strathdon and Mar areas of Aberdeenshire. The clan became one of the 'broken' clans, though the chiefs continued to remain at Inveruglas Castle.

After the proscription had been repealed, John's son, Walter, became the 16th Chief and fought for Charles I under the Marquis of Montrose. When Oliver Cromwell invaded Scotland his Roundheads attacked Inveruglas and set it on fire (this was the second time Cromwell's men attacked the castle). It was eventually abandoned, and a new country house was built at Tarbet on the mainland. The clan seat later moved to Arrochar, where the site of the house is now occupied by the Cobbler Hotel, itself erected in 1697. A ghostly Green Lady, who formerly haunted the original MacFarlane house, now occupies the hotel and has been seen on a number of occasions by guests and hotel employees. She is said to be the spirit of a MacFarlane who was shot and killed by one of the Clan Colquhoun.

19 MacGregor of MacGregor
The Great Leap

Clan Gregor claim descent from the ancient kings of Scotland, and its coat of arms contains an antique crown, with the motto, 'S Rioghal mo dhream, or 'Royal is my race'. From 1603 to 1661 and from 1693 to 1774 the clan was proscribed by the Scottish and British governments. No one was to bear the name MacGregor, under pain of death; any document signed by a MacGregor was declared illegal; and, should anyone kill a MacGregor, their crime was not punishable. James VI's edict stated that the name of MacGregor should be 'altogidder abolisheed', so that all who bore that name had to adopt another or suffer death. Many of the clan adopted names such as Campbell, Douglas, Drummond, Graham, Grant, Murray, Stewart or even Love (the name adopted by my own ancestor). Our tale predates the time of proscription, however, but was partially instrumental in bringing it about.

Gregor Ruadh MacGregor was born sometime in the middle of the sixteenth century, the second son of Alasdair MacGregor of Glenstrae, eighth Chief of the Clan. His mother was born a Campbell of Ardkinglas, and Gregor Ruadh ('red Gregor') was sent to live with the Campbells of Innerwick, in Glen Lyon, who brought him up. He seems to have got on well with the family – indeed, he married Marion, a daughter of his host, Donnachaidh Ruadh na Féileachd, Red Duncan Campbell the Hospitable (d 1578).

In 1560 Gregor Ruadh succeeded to the chiefship on the death of his elder brother – killed by an arrow as he crossed the mountains of Mamlorn from the head of Glen Lyon towards Rannoch Moor. The new Chief asked his relations the Campbells of Glenorchy if he could be given the ancestral MacGregor lands of Glenstrae, which

Chief of MacGregor's coat of arms

lie at the northern end of Loch Awe in Argyll, but 'Grey' Colin Campbell (d 1583) refused. This greatly upset Gregor and caused his clansmen to rally behind him against the Campbells. Grey Colin tried to have bonds of friendship between the two families drawn up, but MacGregor refused to sign them, and he and his clansmen began a ten-year campaign against the Campbells, reiving their cattle and then selling them. He became something of an outlaw, living wild in the hills, and his wife returned to her father's new home of Carnban Castle, which he had built in 1564.

In 1563 Gregor Ruadh became friendly with the young Stewart of Appin, and together they took part in a number of raids against the might of the Campbells. In the same year Grey Colin managed to acquire a charter to the lands of Glenstrae, and commenced his own campaign against Gregor Ruadh. On 22 September Sir John Campbell of Glenorchy received a commission of fire and sword against the clan: no one was to receive or assist any member of the

Clan Gregor, nor supply them in any manner whatsoever with meat, drink or clothing. A later act forbade any members of the clan to assemble in groups of more than four. According to the contemporary 'Chronicle of Fortingall' – written by Sir James MacGregor, Dean of Lismore and included in William Bowie's *Black Book of Taymouth* – 1563 saw 'Ane guid simmer, ane guid hairst, except the Laird of Glenorchy warreth against the MacGregors'. Writing after Grey Colin's death, the Dean noted that he was 'ane great justiciar all his tyme though he sustenit the dedlie feud against the Clan Gregor – notwithstanding his tyranny, his son and successor proved a still worse foe to us.'

At midnight on 11 June 1565 two members of the Clan Gregor were murdered by James MacGelstalcar, or Mac an Stalker Rioch – it is thought, at the instigation of Grey Colin Campbell. MacGelstalcar – the son of a noted archer, and 'a most wicked man and oppressor of the poor', according to the *Chronicle of Fortingall* – was a noted archer himself, and tradition states that he could fire an arrow from one side of Loch Tay to the other. The murdered MacGregors were Gregor MacGregor, son of the Dean of Lismore, and Robert MacConil or MacGregor. Gregor Ruadh decided that he would have to avenge these murders, so on 27 July he made his way to the south side of Loch Tay at Ardeonaig where he found MacGelstalcar, slew the miscreant and raided his home. In the same year the chief of MacGregor joined the Earl of Argyll in Chatelherault's rebellion (for which he received a remission at a later date).

Mary Queen of Scots took an interest in the Clan Gregor and in 1566 ordered that the clan be given part of the Menzies land and stock on the side of Loch Rannoch, so that they were no longer landless, and so would not need to raid their neighbours. Her execution in 1567 resulted in the grant being withdrawn, however, and the persecution continued. In 1569 Grey Colin's men came to Carnban Castle, suspecting that Gregor was inside, visiting his wife. They surrounded the building, and forced entry taking their kinsmen by surprise. Gregor was in bed but heard the noise and managed to escape. Some of the Campbells who remained outside spotted the young chief and set off in pursuit with a pack of bloodhounds. MacGregor ran like a hare down the valley of the Lyon for around three miles, to a spot where the river flowed through a deep gorge. At the narrowest part of the Pass of Lyon, where the two banks of the river were only 24 feet apart, he made a gigantic leap for his life, landed precariously on the opposite bank and managed to scramble up the other side. The pursuers halted at the gorge and none dared emulate the feat. Since that time the spot has become known as MacGregor's Leap.

Gregor Ruadh had made a lucky escape, but the Campbell net drew ever closer. He was eventually captured at Carnban and dragged back to Finlarig Castle at Killin where he was tried. As one would expect, he was found guilty and was sentenced to death. Although there was a beheading pit at Finlarig, he was transported the length of Loch Tay to Balloch Castle (since rebuilt and known as Taymouth Castle), which had been a MacGregor castle until Grey Colin had turned out the old MacGregor laird. There Gregor Ruadh MacGregor was held prisoner for some months before he was beheaded on 7 April 1570. According to an old account, Sir Colin Campbell, 'beheidit the Laird of MacGregour himself at Kenmoir in presence of the Erle of Atholl, the justice clerk, and sundrie other nobillmen', and it is said that Gregor's father-in-law signed the very paper which condemned him to death.

Gregor's widow, Marion, mourned her husband's death for many years. Her grieving inspired a poignant Gaelic elegy, the *Lament for Red Gregor of the White Hand*, part of which translates as:

> Had my Gregor of his clansmen
> Twelve good men and brave,
> I would not now be shedding tears,
> His kin my babe would save.
>
> Ochain, ochain, ochain, darling,
> Sad at heart am I;
> Ochain, ochain, ochain, darling,
> Father hears not our cry.

In August 1570 the Gregarach, as members of the clan were styled in Gaelic, raided the Campbell country around the head of Loch Awe. They destroyed many of the croft houses in the vicinity of Kilchurn Castle, and killed thirteen Campbell men in revenge for their chief's execution.

Gregor Ruadh was succeeded as chief by his son Alasdair, who was only three years old when his father was executed; he grew up to be known as the 'Arrow of Glen Lyon', because of his skill with a bow. Gregor's second son, Iain, known as 'Black John of the Coat of Mail', was killed at the Battle of Glenfruin, when the MacGregors attacked the Colquhouns of Luss. The lack of an active chief, and the government's proscription, left the clan in something of a turmoil, but the 'children of the mist' kept their clan spirit alive.

20 Mackay of Reay
The Scandinavian War Hero

King Gustavus Adolphus, who ruled Sweden from 1611 to 1632, was known as 'invincible' Gustavus, having successfully waged war against Denmark, Russia, Poland and Germany. He was an important leader in the Thirty Years' War, joining the Protestant side in 1630. Much of his strength in battle was due to a regiment in his army that was raised and led by a Scotsman: Donald, chief of Clan Mackay, or Clann Aodh as it is known in Gaelic.

Sir Donald Mackay of Farr and Strathnaver was born around 1591, the son of Hugh Mackay of Farr and Lady Jean Gordon, and grandson of the notable Iye (or Y) Mackay (d 1571), who caused considerable trouble to the Scottish government of Mary Queen of Scots. In 1610, at the age of twenty Donald came to the notice of the authorities and was appointed a Justice of the Peace for Inverness and Cromarty, and for Sutherland also in 1612. When he was 21 he and John Gordon of Embo captured Arthur Smith, a forger employed by the so-called 'wicked' fifth Earl of Caithness; the earl, a noted scoundrel and a murderer, set up a mint to produce false coinage that was circulated throughout the north of Scotland. Mackay and Gordon travelled to Thurso where they found Smith. During the struggle to take him, James Sinclair of Strickage, a nephew of Lord Caithness, tried to effect Smith's release but was killed in the scuffle; in the circumstances, it was felt that Smith had to be executed to prevent his escape. The Earl of Caithness had Mackay tried for murder before the Privy Council. However, he dropped the charges, for fear of implicating himself in the forgery racket, and Mackay and Gordon received a pardon and remission of all charges against them in December 1613. (More on the wild lifestyle of the Earl can be found in Chapter 39.)

There was a feud between the Mackays and the Camerons of
Lochiel, and on 9 December 1613 Donald was one of a number of
notables who received a commission of fire and sword against Allan
MacDonald Dubh Cameron of Lochiel, 16th Chief of that clan.
Cameron was charged with having 'committit most detestable and
cruell murthouris and slauchteris' and 'brynt houssis, cornis, and
barnes, besydis diverse utheris insolencyis.' A reward of one thousand pounds was offered for his capture, but he seems to have
dodged all attempts, dying in 1647.

In 1614 Mackay succeeded his father as clan chief, and in April
1616 went to London, where he was knighted by King James (the
charter for this seems to be lost). In 1618 he and his uncles, Sir
Robert and Sir Alexander Gordon, quarrelled, and Donald decided
to join forces with his former adversaries the Sinclairs in a campaign
against Clan Gunn. He tried to avenge old crimes the Gunns had
committed against the crown, pursuing in particular Alexander and
John Gunn. However, he was later reconciled with his family, and in
1622 was named in a commission of fire and sword against the Earl
of Caithness, head of the Sinclairs.

In 1626 Sir Donald received a commission from Charles I to raise
a troop of three thousand soldiers from the north of Scotland and
take them to Germany to assist Count Mansfeld fighting on the
Protestant side in what has since become known as the Thirty Years
War. This band of men, which consisted of members of the Gordon,
Gunn, Innes, Mackay, Munro, Ross and Sinclair clans, left
Cromarty in October 1626. Mackay, however, was ill and was
unable to go with them. He remained in Britain (and Charles I
granted him a Nova Scotian baronetcy on 28 March 1627), but travelled to Germany as soon as he could, only to find that Mansfeld had
died. He therefore led the Highlanders north to offer their services
to King Christian IV of Denmark. Mackay's men were strong in
battle, and gained the nickname 'The Invincible Regiment', but the
greater forces of the imperialists pushed them back – although
Mackay's regiment held the Pass of Oldenburg for some time. On
his return to Scotland in 1628, Sir Donald was created Lord Reay for
his services. (He would later also have been raised to Earl of
Strathnaver, had the King not been executed in 1649 before the royal
patent was complete.)

One of Mackay's officers was the 18th Chief of the Munros,
Robert Dubh Munro of Foulis, who was in financial difficulty and
had to earn money by joining the regiment. On 10 October 1626 he

raised a company of Munro clansmen and, having joined forces with Mackay's men, set sail from the port of Cromarty for Denmark. The chief became a colonel of horse and foot, and died at the battle of Ulm, in Germany, in 1633. In 1637 one of his soldiers, Robert Monro, published his memoirs, *Monro: His Expedition with the Worthy Scots Regiment (Called MacKeyes Regiment)*, one of the most detailed accounts of the war. In it he noted that the memory of this regiment 'shall never be forgotten, but shall live in spite of time'.

Another member of Mackay's regiment was Angus Roy Gunn. The Privy Council had previously granted Mackay a commission to bring him before it, to be charged with various crimes. However, when Gunn signed up to join the force, Mackay ignored the letter.

Having enrolled more soldiers in his regiment, Lord Reay returned to Denmark, and commanded the successful defence of Stralsund against the full force of the enemy. In 1629 he took his regiment to fight for Gustavus Adolphus, the great king of Sweden. It is said that Mackay's force, which numbered around 13,000 men, was Gustavus's favourite, and he often sent it to carry out the most difficult tasks. Mackay successfully led them at Leipzig in 1631, taking only two hours to capture Marienburg Castle, which was thought to be impregnable. At the battle of Lützen, where Gustavus was killed, the fighting was so bloody that only one tenth of the regiment survived.

In 1629 the Danish king had awarded Lord Reay £3,000, a further £1,000 coming from Charles I, but the cost of supporting an army in Sweden and Britain was so severe that he had to sell much of his land. In 1631 he was charged with treason for alleging that the regiment raised by the third Marquis of Hamilton was not bound for Scandinavia, but that instead Hamilton was proposing to bring down Charles I and claim the crown for himself. Mackay named David Ramsay, an officer in Hamilton's service, as his informer. However, Ramsay vehemently denied any such knowledge, and Mackay challenged him to a duel. To ensure fair play, the matter was referred to a court of chivalry, which appointed that the combat should take place at Tothill Fields, Westminster, under the supervision of the Earls of Lindsey and Arundel. Each contestant was to be armed with a long sword, a short sword, a pike and a dagger. Believing that neither man was fully innocent, the king intervened before the appointed date and had them both locked up in the Tower of London until they gave a sufficient undertaking to keep the peace.

During the time of civil unrest, in 1643, Lord Reay joined the Earl of Sutherland and others on the side of the Covenanters, but his adherence was unsure; a barque heading north with arms and ammunition for his use was captured by the Earl of Marischal at Peterhead, who claimed that Mackay was 'not ane good covenanter'. He did join the Covenanters of the north later, but played no real part in their rising.

Later in the same year Lord Reay again returned to Denmark, where he assembled a regiment in support of Charles I, with his son Angus as colonel. In 1644 he sailed with this force into Newcastle, which he defended against the Scots under Leslie. However, he was captured in October and imprisoned in Edinburgh Castle for almost a year. After Montrose's victory at the Battle of Kilsyth in 1645 he was released along with other royalists. When Montrose later capitulated, times were unsure for Mackay, and he decided to set sail for Denmark once more. He died seven months later in February 1649, perhaps at Copenhagen. His body was brought back to Scotland, where it was laid to rest at the family burial aisle at Kirkiboll, near Tongue.

21 MacKenzie of Kintail
The Seer's Prophecies

The MacKenzies owned much of the central part of the north-west Highlands, within what was the county of Ross and Cromarty (indeed, Cromarty itself was at one time a separate county, being created in the seventeenth century out of the MacKenzies' Black Isle estates). The clan was usually on the side of the crown, which resulted in its gaining new lands, and its chief titles – Baron MacKenzie of Kintail in 1606 and Earl of Seaforth in 1623. The fourth Earl, Kenneth of MacKenzie, adhered to the Jacobite royal house, dying in exile in 1701, which resulted in the attainder of the title. All this had been predicted in the sixteenth century by a local clairvoyant, Coinneach Odhar, or 'sallow' Kenneth MacKenzie, the Brahan Seer.

Just exactly when the Seer lived is not known. Some accounts state that he lived between about 1610 and 1670 and was a contemporary of his namesake, the fourth Earl. Others think that he lived in the sixteenth century, for in January 1578 a Commission of Justice was issued for the apprehension of 'Kenneth, alias Kennoch Owir, principal or leader in the art of magic'. Whichever century he lived in, most accounts agree that he was born at Baile na Chille, near Uig on the island of Lewis, and came to Easter Ross as a servant on the MacKenzie estates; he gained his name of 'Brahan Seer' from Brahan Castle, a seat of the clan.

The Seer was responsible for hundreds of prophecies, many of them recorded by his contemporaries. Some refer to major happenings in Scottish history, such as the Battle of Culloden, whereas others predict great technological advances, such as the construction of the Caledonian Canal. Most of them, though, were of a more local nature, relating to the MacKenzie family, and the most striking was made around 1660. Kenneth Mor, the third Earl of Seaforth, was in Paris on business, and the trip lasted longer than he had predicted. Back home at Brahan his Countess, Lady Isobel, daughter of the Earl of Cromartie, wondered what he was up to, so she sent for the Brahan Seer. She asked him if he could tell her if her husband was safe and well, for she had not even received a letter from him for months. Coinneach asked her where her husband was meant to be, and she replied that he should be in Paris. The Seer held a semi-precious charm stone to his eye and stared intently into it.

'Your husband is alive and well,' he replied. 'He is well and hearty, merry and happy.'

The Countess was relieved to find that her husband had not died abroad.

'With whom is he?' she asked.

'Ask no more, my Lady. Your husband is merry and happy.'

The Countess began to suspect that the Seer was not telling her the full story, and had visions of her husband dallying with attractive French ladies. She kept pressing Coinneach, and at length he replied,

'Your Lord is in a magnificent room, in very fine company, and far too agreeably employed at the moment to think of yourself. On his knee is a fair lady, his arm around her waist, and her hand pressed to his lips.'

The Countess was outraged, and accused the Seer of defaming her husband, abusing her hospitality and sullying the good name of her lord in the very hall of his castle.

'You shall suffer the most signal vengeance I can inflict – you shall suffer the death.'

Coinneach Odhar was dismayed at this reaction, for her anger should have been directed not at him but at her husband. He pulled out his magic stone once more, and looked into it.

I see far into the future and I read the doom of the race of my oppressor. The long-descended line of Seaforth will, ere many generations have passed, end in extinction and sorrow. I see a chief, the last of his house, both deaf and dumb. He will be the father of four fair sons, all of whom he will follow to the tomb. He will live careworn and die mourning, knowing that the honours of his line are to be extinguished forever, and that no future chief of the MacKenzies shall bear rule at Brahan or in Kintail. After lamenting over the last and most promising of his sons, he himself shall sink into the grave, and the remnant of his possessions shall be inherited by a white-coifed lassie from the east, and she is to kill her sister. And as a sign by which it may be known that these things are coming to pass, there shall be four great lairds in the last days of the deaf and dumb Seaforth – Gairloch, Chisholm, Grant and Raasay – of whom one shall be buck-toothed, another hare-lipped, another half-witted, and the fourth a stammerer.

The Seer then threw his magic stone into a nearby lochan and presented himself for execution. This took place at Chanonry Point, near Fortrose, where he was placed in a tar barrel and burnt to death for witchcraft. For a long time a boulder known as 'Coinneach Odhar's Stone' stood at the place, but this was later removed. The site of the execution is now occupied by some bungalows near the lighthouse, and a more modern memorial stands nearby.

According to some local accounts, the Earl of Seaforth tried to prevent the killing of the Seer. He rode out to Chanonry Point, but his horse fell on the way, and he had to run the last half-mile on foot. As he neared the execution site the tar was alight, and the Seer half-dead.

'I tried to save you,' he yelled.

'I know,' Coinneach Odhar replied. 'I could see you coming, but I knew that you would be too late. For what your lady wife has done to me today, your line will end, but mine will only begin. When I am dead a child of my seed will be born on the lands of Brahan, and will be known as the Brahan Child. There will be a Brahan Child in every generation who will see as I can see. Let those beware who would do them harm, for my shadow shall be watching over them.'

The predicted downfall of the MacKenzies duly occurred. The last Earl of Seaforth was Francis Humberston MacKenzie, born in 1755. According to the prediction, the Chief of the MacKenzies who was to suffer all the Seer had foretold was to be deaf and dumb, but Francis was in full possession of his faculties. It was not until late in life that these disabilities began to show. He became deaf as a result of scarlet fever, and in the final two years of his life this affected his speech also. According to Sir Walter Scott, in one of his letters, 'His state was truly pitiable; – all his fine faculties lost in paralytic imbecility, and yet not entirely so but that he perceived his deprivation as in a glass darkly. Sometimes he was fretful and anxious because he did not see his son; sometimes he expostulated and complained that his boy had been allowed to die without his seeing him; and, sometimes, in a less clouded state of intellect, he was sensible of, and lamented his loss in its fullest extent.'

Memorial to the Hon. Caroline MacKenzie

Lord Seaforth had four sons, one of whom died young, but the three survivors all predeceased their father, and, as he began to recall the ancient Seaforth legend, it is said that Francis became more and more withdrawn. The four great lairds who were to be the signs foretold by the Seer were known to him. They were Sir Hector MacKenzie of Gairloch, who had a buck tooth; William Chisholm,

24th Chief of the clan, who had a hare-lip; James Grant of Grant, who was thought of as half-witted in the district, and suffered a lingering illness before his death; and MacLeod of Raasay, who had a stammer. Lord Seaforth died on 11 January 1815.

According to the Seer, of Francis's two daughters, one was to be a white-coifed lassie who would kill her sister. This turned out to be true. In 1823 the heiress of the estates, the Honourable Mary MacKenzie, married Sir Samuel Hood KB, one of the Commissioners for Trinidad and MP for Westminster in 1806. When Sir Samuel died, Lady Hood returned from the Caribbean dressed in mourning clothes (which were white, as was the custom in that part of the world), complete with a 'coif' or hood – significantly, of course, her surname was 'Hood'. Mary remarried in 1817, to James Stewart, third son of the sixth Earl of Galloway, who adopted the surname Stewart-MacKenzie and settled on the Seaforth estates.

Although the island of Lewis was sold to the Mathesons, the Ross-shire estates were virtually complete, and there was no sign of Mary Stewart-MacKenzie killing her sister, the Honourable Caroline MacKenzie. Nonetheless, as predicted, Mary was responsible for Caroline's death. One day they were out in a pony and trap, driving through the Brahan policies. As they passed through a wood something seems to have frightened the ponies, which set off at high speed, and Mrs Stewart-MacKenzie was unable to bring them to a halt. When they came to a junction each pony decided to go a different way, the trap was overturned, and the sisters were thrown out. Both were injured, but Mary recovered, while Caroline died of her injuries soon afterwards. A monument at the road junction commemorates the accident.

22 Mackintosh of Moy
Flood and Feast

The Mackintosh clan is centred on Strathdearn and Strathnairn, and the clan seat was for many years at Moy. The clan is a branch of Clan Chattan, and the chiefs of Mackintosh held the chiefship of Chattan from 1291 – when Angus, the sixth Chief, married Eva, heiress of Chattan – until 1938, when Alfred Mackintosh, 28th Chief of both clans, died without a male heir. Our tale concerns Malcolm Mackintosh, tenth Chief, who lived in the fifteenth century. He was known as Malcolm Beag, or Little Malcolm (but sometimes these nicknames were given in jest, and he may have been quite a large man!).

Malcolm inherited the chiefship from his nephew, Ferquhar Mackintosh, who abdicated the title in 1409. It was not uncommon for the chiefship of a clan to pass in this way, for it was felt that weaker chiefs should relinquish the title to a stronger member of the family. Malcolm was a wise choice. In 1411 he was in command of the Clan Chattan at the Battle of Harlaw in Aberdeenshire, where he fought with the Lord of the Isles. He later took part in the Lord of the Isles' rebellion in the west, but, as the King advanced into Lochaber he changed sides and joined James I to defeat the Lord of the Isles. His support for the crown was rewarded in 1428 when he was appointed Constable of Inverness Castle, and in 1431 when he was granted the lands of Alasdair or Alexander of Lochaber, uncle of the Lord of the Isles. Having made peace with the Lord of the Isles in the 1440s, he was confirmed in his Lochaber lands by the Lord, and granted the office of Bailiary of the district.

Malcolm married Mora MacDonald, a daughter of Clanranald of Moidart. To keep her house she brought some members of the MacQueen clan with her, including one Revan MacMulmor

MacAngus MacQueen, and they eventually settled in the district at Corrybrough Beag. This Revan was with Malcolm when he fought at Harlaw, and the MacQueens of Corrybrough are often referred to as Clan Revan. This clan became a sept of Clan Chattan.

During Malcolm's time as chief, the Cumming, or Comyn, family had occupied the lands of Geddes and Rait, which lie just over two miles south of the town of Nairn. These lands, which anciently belonged to the Geddes family, had long since been acquired by the Mackintoshes, although since the early fourteenth century they had been held by the acquisitive Comyns, who also held other Mackintosh lands in Lochaber, and thus were natural enemies of the clan.

The chief of the Comyns had been appointed Keeper of Inverness Castle, and so had the King's authority in the district. It is said that he had a number of Mackintosh men hanged 'for very slight cause' at a spot thereafter known as Cnoc na Gillean, or 'hill of the lads', which lies on the lands of Skenepark, near Nairn. The lost lands of Geddes and Rait still rankled, and this loss of good clansmen brought the Mackintosh blood to the boil. A group of Mackintoshes burst into Nairn Castle where the Comyns were feasting. In the ensuing fight, all the Comyns were slaughtered, and the Mackintoshes slipped back across the moors to their Highland fastness. It is said that Malcolm Mackintosh himself was present at the attack on the castle, though other accounts do not name him.

Greatly angered by the attack, the Comyns gathered together 1,800 followers at their clan seat and set off for Strathdearn, where the Mackintosh chief had his castle at Moy. Word came from a look-out that the Comyns were on their way, and that they outnumbered the 400 Mackintoshes. Chief Malcolm, wondering how best to defend his lands against such numbers, reckoned that he would be better placed to fend off an attack if he occupied the islet in the middle of Loch Moy, where there was a small fortress. Accordingly, he and his clansmen thus made their way to the island by boat.

The Comyns came over the Moor of Cawdor and arrived at Castle Moy, to discover that the building was empty. They began a search of the area, and noticed the islet in the loch and the many people taking refuge there. They realised that there would be too many of them to be overcome by the number of men they could ferry across at any one time, so they sat down to think out a plan of attack. It was decided that the best method would be to starve the Mackintoshes out – and to speed the process they set about raising the water level in the loch by building a dam across its foot, where the waters emptied into the Funlack Burn. The 1,800 men worked quickly, using boulders and turfs to block the escaping waters, as well as timbers taken from nearby crofthouses. The islet was a fairly low one, and it did not require much of a rise in the water level to reduce its surface area and flood the building that stood on it.

At first the Mackintoshes were unaware that the island was getting smaller, but they began to panic as soon as the waters rose enough to soak all their provisions. Action was required, but no one was sure just what to do. It was eventually decided to wait until nightfall, when a clansman slipped out of the island refuge on the smallest boat, rowed slowly and silently across the loch to the dam and managed to destroy it. (According to one old account, he bored holes in the planks and blocked them again with plugs which he attached to strings. When he pulled all the strings at once, the water gushed out with such force as to wash away the remainder of the dam.) Many of the Comyn forces were camped downstream of the dam, and the sudden rush of escaping water engulfed their camp-site and caused much damage to their belongings. (It is also said that the Mackintosh who destroyed the dam also died, because the waters dragged his boat with the flow, capsized it and drowned him.)

The Mackintoshes then made their escape from the flooded islet, landed on the shore of the loch and hid themselves in the woods to await the Comyns. They encountered a force of the latter, which had been sent round the loch to search for the dam-busters, on the shore of the loch, and a battle ensued. Some of the Mackintoshes fled over the hill, as though trying to escape. A group of Comyns pursued them, but the Mackintoshes turned and managed to kill most of them. The dead Comyns were buried beneath cairns of stones which long after marked their graves.

A tradition in the district claims that the Comyns later invited the Mackintoshes to a feast in Rait Castle, at which it was proposed to settle their differences by fairer means. The Mackintoshes, though suspicious of their hosts' intentions, agreed and accepted the invitation. They were right to be wary, for the chief of Comyn's daughter overheard plans for a slaughter. The meal was to take place in the great hall of the castle, and the diners were to be seated round a large trestle table, Mackintosh and Comyn alternately. At a signal (the cook bringing in a bull's head) the Comyns would murder the Mackintoshes. However, the Comyn girl had a Mackintosh boyfriend – a liaison she had to keep secret, because of the feud. Not knowing whether he would be invited to the feast, she decided that she must warn him of what was about to happen. They met that evening at their secret trysting place at the Grey Stone of Croy, an ancient standing stone. To ease her conscience about giving information to the enemy, the lad stood at one side of the stone, and the girl at the other, and she told her worries to the stone – knowing full well that her boyfriend would overhear.

When the great feast in Rait Castle was held the meal went well, and the Comyns became more relaxed as time passed, thinking that their plans were going well. When the hall door opened, though, and the bull's head was presented on a silver platter, the Mackintoshes were the quicker; they produced their dirks from beneath their cloaks and slew their hosts. But somehow (tradition does not relate how) the Comyn chief survived, and he blamed his daughter for revealing the plans. The pair argued in the upper floors of the castle, and in the ensuing struggle, her father cut off her hands with a swipe of his broadsword, and she fell to her death from the battlements. It is said that the girl's spirit, dressed in bloodstained garments, still roams around the castle.

The feud between the Mackintoshes and Comyns was eventually settled, and Malcolm Mackintosh received a charter for the lands of Geddes and Rait in 1442. He died either in 1457 or 1464 (accounts vary) and was succeeded by his eldest son, Duncan Mackintosh.

23 Maclaine of Lochbuie
The Ugly Woman

The names Maclean and Maclaine are often confused. This is not a great problem, however, for they are both branches of the same family. The original spelling seems to have been Maclean, and this is the version still used by the Macleans of Duart. Their distant cousins, the Maclaines of Lochbuie, use the variant spelling, but did not do so until the eighth chief, Hector, decided to adopt it in the sixteenth century. Although both families are now regarded as separate clans in their own right, the Macleans of Duart are regarded as the senior branch of the family, being descended from Lachlan Lubanach, son of Iain Dubh MacGillemoir Maclean. The ancestor of the Maclaines was Lachlan's brother, Eachin Reganach – but this family claims that he was the elder brother, and therefore it should be the senior.

The feud between the Macleans and Maclaines has existed for many centuries, and there are many tales of the battles between them. At one time they were on friendly terms, and it was the custom for the best man of each clan to be used to send messages to and fro between their castles. However, one day Lochbuie sent a message and the man never returned. This act of treachery resuscitated the feud, and the two families refused to speak to each other. After a time relations improved, and the lady of Lochbuie was able to visit Duart Castle. When she was ready to leave she requested Maclean's best man to accompany her back over the rough track to Lochbuie. Crossing a burn near the head of Loch Spelve, her shoelaces became loose, and she asked the man if he would please retie them. As he bent down to do so, she drew a dirk and stabbed him in the back.

At one time Ewen Maclaine tried to overthrow his father and

claim the chiefship of Lochbuie for himself. Old John (or Iain), fifth Chief of Lochbuie, known as the 'toothless', had to enlist the help of his distant kinsman, Hector Maclean of Duart, to deal with the threat – and Duart was only too glad to help, being keen to take over the Lochbuie lands. Ewen was killed in a battle against his father at the head of Glen Forsa in 1538, his head cut from his body by a blow from a Lochaber axe. His frightened horse galloped up to the head of the glen, Ewen's headless corpse still slumped on its back, until near the waterfalls of Glen Lussa, the corpse fell off (a small cairn was later raised on the spot). In some versions of the tale, Ewen was riding amongst the hills of Mull on the evening before the battle, when he came across a cailleach, or old woman, busy washing clothes in a mountain stream. As he came closer he noticed that the garments she was washing were shirts, and that they were covered in blood – he then realised that what he saw was a herald of death, a ghostly figure foretelling death in battle.

Ewen was thereafter known as Eoghan a' Chinn Bhig (Ewen the little-head), and it is said that his headless ghost still roams Mull on horseback, manifesting most often just before the death of a Lochbuie chief. A gravestone on the island of Iona is said to mark his last resting place. A long tapering slab, it is decorated with Celtic knotwork, a claymore, wild beasts and a man on horseback. Sir Walter Scott used the tale of Ewen in his epic poem, *The Lady of the Lake*:

> Sounds, too, had come in midnight blast
> Of charging steed, careering fast
> Along Ben Talla's shingly side,
> Where mortal horseman ne'er might ride.

Having dealt with the heir, Hector Maclean of Duart decided that he would do away with Old John Maclaine, and thus claim the estates. He could not bring himself to kill him, however, and decided instead to have him imprisoned on the remote island of Carn na Burgh Mor, one of the Treshnish Isles. It was only a few acres in size, but there was a castle on it and sufficient grazing for a few cows (the castle had been granted to the Macleans of Duart in 1493 when the Lordship of the Isles was forfeited; it passed into royal hands, but in 1514 Lachlan Maclean of Duart seized the fortress and kept a small garrison there). After Hector's followers had captured Old John and tied him up, Hector asked if he had any requests before he was taken

Ewen Maclaine's gravestone, Iona

by boat to the island. Lochbuie asked for the services of a woman, to cook and clean for him, whilst he was imprisoned on the island. Maclean agreed. However, he feared that Maclaine would use the woman to bear him a new heir, and to prevent this, he arranged for the ugliest woman on the island of Mull to be sent to the islet as housekeeper. The pair were taken to the island and put ashore; without the use of a boat they were trapped, as if in prison. They spent a number of seasons on the island, and in time Maclaine fell in love with the ugly woman, and she became pregnant. The Macleans were incensed at this and took the woman back to Mull, where a midwife was appointed to look after her and given strict instructions to inform the chief if the child should be male – if so, he was to be killed.

The woman gave birth to a daughter, and the midwife, relieved that the child could live, ran from the croft to announce that its life could be spared. An hour or so later, however, a twin son was born, and realising that his life was in immediate danger, the woman's family arranged for her and the child to be taken to a secret cave on the slopes of Beinn Mhor, where a clansman and his five (some accounts say seven) sons looked after them.

Word leaked out to Maclean of Duart that Old Lochbuie had succeeded in producing an heir, and he sent soldiers to the lands of Lochbuie to search out the child and kill him. A reward was offered to anyone willing to reveal where he was hidden, or to name those who knew where the place of concealment was, and within a few months someone had told the chief the names of the family who cared for the infant heir. Maclean's men searched out the shieling where the family lived, but the father refused to reveal the infant's hiding-place. As his sons returned one by one to the shieling from their work with the cattle, they were similarly questioned. Each refused to tell, and each was beheaded in full view of his father. At length all the sons were killed, and the old man was asked what he thought now.

'At least I can die happy,' he replied, 'knowing that all my sons were faithful to the cause.'

The soldiers then killed him in anger. The shieling where the family lived was thereafter known as Airigh na Sliseig, or 'shieling of the slicing', from the fact the heads of the victims were sliced from their bodies.

The young Maclaine survived and was brought up by another member of the clan. He was known as Murchadh Gearr, or

Murdoch the Stunted, probably on account of a disability inherited from his mother. When Iain the Toothless died in 1494 Murdoch's mother told him who his real father had been, and that he was the rightful chief of Lochbuie. She also warned him that he would have to flee the island. He therefore went to the northern shores of Ireland and remained there for a year and a day, before returning to Mull with twelve strong companions to claim back his rightful territory. They made their way to the castle of Lochbuie, and Murdoch managed to identify himself to his former nurse, who was inside the building. With her assistance, he and his men took the castle and put its usurper, Murdoch of Scallasdale to flight. (At a later date Murdoch Gearr attacked Murdoch of Scallasdale at Grulin and defeated him.) Murdoch was legitimated in 1538 and managed to reclaim Lochbuie, his descendants holding the lands until the 1920s.

24 Maclean of Duart
The Lady's Rock

Many visitors who take the ferry across the Firth of Lorne to the 'Dark Island' of Mull are impressed by the sturdy outline of Duart Castle, standing on one of the island's easternmost promontories. The castle seems to grow out of the rock headland, its thick walls protecting the residents not only from attacks but also from the driving rain and wind which can be experienced on the west coast of Scotland. Duart has been the seat of the chiefs of Maclean for many centuries, apart from a few modern decades, when the castle went out of their control. It was repurchased in 1911 by Sir Fitzroy Maclean and restored, both as a family seat and clan centre.

On the starboard side of the ferry, the travellers' attention is drawn to the lighthouse off the southern end of the island of Lismore, erected in 1833 by Robert Stevenson to guide seamen around dangerous rocks and to act as a guidepost at the junction of four sea-routes – the Lynn of Morvern, the Lynn of Lorne, the Firth of Lorne and the Sound of Mull. Less often noticed, however, is the Lady's Rock, which lies between Lismore and Mull. A beacon helps to make the rock more obvious, for at high tide little of its surface is visible above water, and, when storms are lashing the waves over it, it can be a major hazard in these treacherous waters.

In the first quarter of the sixteenth century Lachlan Cattanach Maclean was the chief of the Macleans. He became the tenth Chief in 1513, when his father, Hector, died on the battlefield of Flodden. Lachlan was one of the main supporters of the claim by Sir Donald MacDonald of Lochalsh to the Lordship of the Isles, and was responsible for seizing the castles of Carn na Burgh Mor and Dunskaich in 1513. Later persuaded to support the government by the Earl of Argyll, he arrested two of Sir Donald's brothers and

The Lady's Rock

requested a free remission of all his offences, as well as those of his 'kin, men, servants and part-takers', declaring that Sir Donald should be denounced as a traitor and his two brothers executed according to law. Lachlan's appeal succeeded for he was acquitted of all crimes in 1517.

Lachlan married Lady Catherine (or, according to some accounts, Elizabeth) Campbell, daughter of the second Earl of Argyll, as his second wife (his first had also been a Campbell: Margaret, daughter of the Auchinbreck branch of the clan). The marriage was a happy one to start with, and the link with the all-powerful Campbells of Argyll was useful, for they would take the side of Maclean in any of the feuds they got involved in. However, after a few years had passed, Lachlan began to fret about his wife, for she had failed to produce the much-wanted heir. Lachlan was beginning to get old, and he despaired of ever having a son to succeed to the castle and lands. So he planned to get rid of her, and search for a new and younger wife – but most of the different methods of doing away with her that he thought of were too risky, for he did not want to get caught and face the wrath of the Campbells. He needed to think of some scheme that would look like an accident, so that the Campbells would shower him with pity, and he would be free to search for another wife.

There were also tales of strange behaviour on the part of his wife: it was said that she had tried to poison her husband, and that she had a lover – a man who spent most of his time practising as a monk, but who was a regular visitor to Lady Catherine, and whose behaviour on these visits was anything but religious.

One day, while crossing to the mainland, Lachlan noticed the rock halfway between Mull and Lismore (if it had a name at that time, it has long-since been forgotten). He hatched a plan, and one day arranged for his wife to cross with him to Argyll; it was a misty day, and no-one noticed that Maclean's galley was anchored off the barren rock. Lachlan and two of his vassals grabbed his wife, tied her hands behind her back and forced her into a rowing boat which took her the short distance to the rock. Her hands were tied to a stake that had been hammered into a fissure to prevent her breaking free and perhaps swimming to safety, freezing cold though the waters were. With a gag in her mouth, Lady Catherine was unable to scream for help as Lachlan and his accomplices returned to their galley.

Maclean sailed on and anchored in Oban Bay. He reckoned that by this time the tide would have risen, and his wife would have drowned. He arranged for a runner to head south to Inveraray Castle to notify Campbell of Argyll that Lady Catherine had fallen overboard and that despite their attempts to rescue her, they had been unable to locate her in the mist. For the next few days Maclean acted the grieving widower. He lowered his standard on the castle ramparts, and spent much of his time alone, supposedly mourning his loss.

There was a flaw in Maclean's scheme, however. He did not reckon on a passing fishing boat coming upon the tied-up woman. Perhaps she had managed to lower the gag and call for help before the waves covered most of the rock. (Other accounts claim that she was rescued by some Macleans, for Lachlan was not a well-liked chief, and at one time senior members of the family had met to try and oust him from the chiefship.) At any rate, she was saved, and her rescuers took her to the mainland. She quickly made her way to Inveraray where she related her tale to her brother.

Incensed at his sister's treatment and Maclean's attempt to murder her, the brother plotted revenge. He did not want to attack Duart Castle, for the casualties on both sides would be too great. He bided his time, waiting until Lachlan was away from his home-land – indeed he must have waited some considerable time, for in the meanwhile Lachlan Maclean married a third wife, Marian Maclean, daughter of the Captain of Carn na Burgh Mor. (He was unlucky in love yet again, for she is said to have become rather too well acquainted with an Irish chieftain by the name of William O'Buie – although she did provide Lachlan with the much-longed for heir, Hector, and a second son, Allan, for good measure.)

In 1524 Lachlan Maclean had to go to Edinburgh on business. He travelled across country, and there was every chance he called at Inveraray Castle to meet his 'late' wife's family (if so, Lady Catherine was kept hidden whilst he was there). Behind the scenes the Campbells meanwhile plotted their revenge. One of their men followed Maclean to the capital, and that night, 10 November, while sleeping at a city inn, he was 'dirked in bed' (stabbed with the Highland dirk, or dagger). Who was responsible for the act of revenge is not certain, but most accounts claim that it was the Earl of Argyll's brother, Sir John Campbell – styled by some Campbell of Achallader, by others Campbell of Calder (or Cawdor), for he had married Muriel Calder, heiress of that estate, in 1510.

When news of Lachlan Maclean's murder reached Mull his clansmen instantly armed themselves and prepared to invade Argyll. The Campbells likewise got ready for an anticipated attack, but the Scottish government managed to intervene, and no bloodshed took place. However, five years later, the Macleans joined the MacDonalds of Islay in their feud with the Campbells, and attacked the lands of Roseneath and Craignish, ravaging the countryside and killing many of its inhabitants. The Campbells retaliated soon afterwards, destroying many homes and killing a number of their occupants throughout Mull, Tiree and that part of Morvern belonging to the Macleans. In May 1530 the next Lachlan Maclean and Alasdair MacDonald of Islay made their personal submissions to King James V at Stirling and, on receipt of security for their obedience, were pardoned.

The Scottish poet, Thomas Campbell (1777–1844), better known for poems such as 'Ye Mariners of England' and 'Lord Ullin's Daughter', wrote one entitled 'Glenara' which is based on the story of the Lady's Rock. A nineteenth-century tragedy by a Miss Baillie, *The Family Legend*, was also based on the tale.

25 MacLeod of Dunvegan
The Fairy Lullaby

Dunvegan Castle on Skye, perched on a rock overlooking the tidal Loch Dunvegan, is a magical place. At one time the only entrance to the castle was through the sea gate which led directly to the shore, where the chief's galley would be anchored, but in the eighteenth century a new landward entrance was created, for by that time the island was peaceful, and clan feuds had subsided.

A number of traditional tales are associated with the castle. The most famous is the story of the fairy flag, or Am Bratach Sith as it is known in Gaelic; another tale recounts how Sir Rory Mor MacLeod (d 1626), the 13th Chief, acquired the hunting horn which still hangs in the castle. A third, which we will now relate in more detail, concerns the traditional fairy lullaby.

It is said that in the late thirteenth century the third chief, Malcolm, grandson of Leoid or Leod, and his wife, a daughter of the Earl of Mar, had a son and heir, Iain (John), a bonny and cheerful lad. He was their pride and joy, and all the MacLeod clansmen were proud of their future chief. One day the child's nanny entered the upper room in Dunvegan Castle where the baby had been left sleeping. She was horrified to discover that the cradle was empty, the covers ruffled and the baby gone. Screaming, she ran down to the great hall where she announced that the heir of MacLeod was missing. A number of important MacLeod clansmen were gathered there, and within a very short time they instituted a thorough search of the castle. No trace of the child was discovered, so the search was extended to cover the grounds and the neighbourhood. There was a tradition on Skye of infants being taken by golden eagles or foxes, but the gamekeepers who knew where these creatures made their homes found no trace of the child. Suspicion fell upon neighbouring

Dunvegan Castle

clans who had feuded with the MacLeods on and off over the years, but none was willing to admit to stealing the heir. The chief of the MacDonalds, who also lived on Skye, was incensed at the suggestion, replying that 'the MacDonald does not make war with babies'.

As time passed hope of finding the infant MacLeod began to fade. Of all the many theories and suspicions about who or what had stolen the child, none turned out to be correct when followed up. The MacLeod parents began to return to their everyday life, although nursing a sadness that they would never see their beautiful child again.

Come the spring the young ladies of the island set off for their stint at the shielings, to look after the cattle at their summer pasture. One of them was a MacCrimmon, daughter of the MacLeod's piper. After her day's work with the cattle she churned some butter and sat down to mend her skirt, which had been ripped on a sharp boulder. As she sat sewing she became aware of a quiet tune, and, as she listened more closely, she realised that it was a song. What is more, it seemed to be coming from the ground. The lass took her needle and stuck it into the ground and, pulling the thread tight, held it to her ear, so that the taut thread transferred the sound from the earth. Listening intently, she could now make out the words of the song, and she was amazed to discover that it was a lullaby that told of the taking of the baby Iain and his subsequent care by the little people. The girl realised that the spot where she was sitting was next to an ancient dun, and that the little people must be living in it, underground.

The girl ran from the shieling back to Dunvegan Castle, where the MacLeod chief and his lady were amazed to hear what she had found out, and entranced by the words of the lullaby which she sang to them. They sent for their local seers and asked what they could do to get their son back from the fairies. They were told that there was little they could do but bide their time and wait till All Hallows Eve. That night, so tradition said, the fairies left their duns and danced with merriment in the evening moonlight – and that would give the MacLeod men a chance to enter the dun and rescue the heir.

At Hallowe'en a party of strong MacLeod clansmen followed the MacCrimmon lass back up the hillside to the shieling. They found the dun on the side of the hill and made their way inside its old, ruined walls. There they discovered the child, safe and sound, lying in a makeshift cot, and with him was an old woman, whom the fairies had kidnapped to look after him. The men gathered up the child in his cot-cover of the finest silk and returned to Dunvegan carrying him in a large basket on their shoulders, with the pipes playing and the standards waving in the evening light. And as they marched they sang the sweet song of the fairy lullaby.

From that day on, the lullaby was known to the MacLeod nannies, and any new nanny had to learn it. It is lengthy, and the words seem not to mean anything, but Alexander Carmichael translated it into English. The first verse is as follows:

My little Dun Buck thou,
Offspring of the lowing cow,
For whom the Mull cow lows,
My darling and my fair one,
My soul and my delight.
Thou art not of the race of Clan Donald,
But of a race nearer to us –
The race of Leod of the Galleys,
The race of the weighty saplings,
The race of the breast-plates,
Norway was thy patrimony.

The present Fairy Flag, which hangs in the drawing room of the castle, is said to be the cot-cover which was taken from the dun to wrap the child in. There are many other traditions associated with this banner, but most authorities now think that it may have come from the Middle East, rather than from fairyland. It may have been some form of holy relic, perhaps a shroud or shirt belonging to one of the early saints from the Holy Land. It seems to have made its way to Constantinople, for it was there that it was acquired by Harald Haardrade, the Viking crusader known as 'Hard Counsel', who then took it back to Scandinavia. The 'shirt' became his lucky banner – each time he waved it in war his fortune changed, and he always seemed to win – and so he named it Landoda, or 'land ravisher'. When Harald Haardrade invaded England in 1066 he had the banner with him when he fought King Harold of England at the Battle of Stamford Bridge. The battle was going against the Vikings, and as Harald tried to unfurl his 'land ravisher' he was killed by an arrow. One of his men, Godred Crovan, managed to rescue the banner and escaped with it to the Western Isles, which he conquered and set himself up as King of the Isles. His sons succeeded him: first Lagmadr, the elder, and then Olaf the Black; it is Olaf's son, Leod, who is reckoned to be the progenitor of the MacLeods of Dunvegan. Thus the Fairy Flag is likely to be the very same lucky banner used by Vikings and originally acquired as a saintly relic in Constantinople.

The Fairy Flag is said to have brought good luck in battle to the MacLeods also, and to have had the magical ability to rescue the clan when it was on the losing side in a conflict. It was usually carried into battle furled, but if all hope of victory seemed lost, the banner was unfurled, and a miraculous turnaround in MacLeod fortunes ensued. According to some accounts, such rescues can happen only three times, and two of these 'lives' have been used – at the Battle of Glendale in about 1490, and at the Battle of Trumpan in 1580.

There are tales of other occasions when the banner was unfurled. It is said to have been used to prevent a plague that killed many cattle on Skye, and, less worthily, it was unfurled in 1799, when, in the absence of Norman MacLeod, 23rd Chief, the estate factor, Hector MacDonald Buchanan, and an English blacksmith forced open the iron chest in which it was stored. The latter incident was predicted by Kenneth MacKenzie, the Brahan Seer, and as a result the heir to the chiefship drowned at sea when his ship, *H.M.S. Queen Charlotte*, was blown up.

The Iain MacLeod who was stolen by the fairies (d *c* 1392) became the fourth Chief of the MacLeods on the death of his father around 1360. Some say that he later married the fairy princess who had stolen him years before, but in her elder years she started longing for her fairy homeland. She announced that she wished to 'go home', and Iain agreed to walk with her to a spot between Dunvegan and Waternish where three rivers and three roads meet, and there they parted. The spot has been known ever since as the Fairy Bridge.

26 MacNab of MacNab
The Head of Neish

For many years the Neishes and MacNabs feuded over the high ground between Loch Earn and Loch Tay in Perthshire. The MacNabs had their castle at Ellanryne, or Eilean Ran, at the west end of Loch Tay near the present village of Killin. The castle, of which there is now no trace, stood on a promontory between the rivers Lochay and Dochart and was frequently surrounded by water when the rivers burst their banks.

The Neishes, or MacNeishes as they are sometimes styled, were a branch of the MacGregors – although some claim that they were descended from Naoise, who came to Scotland from Ireland with his lover Deirdre, around the same time as the Celtic saints Fillan, Drostan and Kessog. They lived around St Fillans, at the east end of Loch Earn. They had no great castle, but they did have a stronghold on a little islet in the loch, called Eilean nan Naoiseach (the Neishes' Island), at Port Mor, near St Fillans. Formerly a crannog, or lake-dwelling, it had been adapted as a place of refuge in time of trouble.

A battle is said to have taken place between the two clans in Gleann Bualtachan, between St Fillans and Comrie, in 1522. A smaller force of Neishes, led by an aged chief, was defeated by the MacNabs. The Neish chief fought courageously and, it is said, he was only overpowered when three MacNab soldiers leapt on him from behind, lunging from a great boulder called Clach Mhor. According to tradition, MacCallum Glas, the Neish bard, composed a poem on this defeat in which he placed a curse on the Clach Mhor. Since that day dogs are frightened to go near the boulder: their hairs stand on end and they start growling for no apparent reason.

MacNab chief's insignia

Many of the Neishes were killed in this battle, and few males survived. After it, they spent most of their nights on the island, only coming ashore during the daytime to tend their cattle. The clan held a grudge against the MacNabs, and constantly plotted to seek their revenge.

It is said that in December 1612 the MacNabs were preparing for the New Year festivities, and made a list of provisions needed for the great feast that was to be held in their castle. The list was a long one, and included a number of bottles of fine wines, for they were tired of drinking the whisky which they distilled themselves. Armed with the list, and some money, servants from the MacNab castle set off for the weekly market in Crieff. Their route crossed the hills towards Loch Earn, following drove roads that led up the glen behind Ardeonaig, down Glen Beich and then via Loch Earn and Comrie to Crieff. From their island stronghold the Neishes spotted the MacNab servants passing along the side of the loch and, surmising that they were heading for the market, made plans to rob them on their return. A couple of nights later look-outs spotted the MacNabs coming back up Strathearn. Word was quickly relayed to the chief, who positioned his men on the hillside above the road. As the MacNab men passed, heavily laden with delicacies and wine, the Neishes fell upon them, and, taken by surprise, the MacNabs dropped their provisions and fled.

Back at Loch Tay, the MacNabs' elderly chief, Finlay, was outraged. He sent for his twelve sons, told them what had happened and, in Gaelic, he uttered the phrase which was to become well known throughout the Highlands, ''S i an oidhche an oidhche, nam b'iad na gillean na gillean' ('tonight is the night, if the lads were the lads'). The hint was quickly taken, and the MacNab sons prepared for a foray into Neish territory. They armed themselves with dirks, claymores and the odd pistol and set off from Killin in a rowing-boat. They rowed the five or so miles down the loch to Ardeonaig, where they landed, and then, with six men on each side, carried the boat up the glen, over the watershed and down Glen Beich. Where the burn flows into Loch Earn they relaunched their boat and rowed eastwards for four and a half miles to Eilean nan Naoiseach.

The eldest son, Iain Min Mac an Aba, or smooth John MacNab, landed on the island and strode up to the door of the Neish stronghold. It was by now the middle of the night, and his thunderous knocking echoed over the frosty loch. The old chief of the Neishes, roused from his sleep, called from a window, 'Who is there?'

'Who would you least like it to be?' answered Iain Min.

Old Neish thought for a short while, then remembered the deeds of his men that day.

'Smooth Iain MacNab,' he replied.

'If he has been smooth until now,' answered Iain, 'then tonight he will be rough.'

By this time the rest of the MacNabs had gathered outside the Neish house, and they battered the door down and found many of the Neish family and servants struggling up from sleep – the fire was still smouldering on the hearth, and empty wine bottles and the remains of the MacNab provisions were strewn around the floor.

The Neish's drunken condition meant that they were easily defeated in the struggle that ensued. The MacNabs killed everyone they found, and it is said that the water which surrounded the islet was dyed red with blood. The chief of the Neishes had his head severed from his body by a great blow from a claymore, and the trophy was wrapped in a plaid and taken back to the MacNab boat. The sole survivor of the massacre was a young boy, MacIldowie, grandson of the chief, whose mother had hidden him in a dark corner; when the Abbot of Innerpeffray came to Loch Earn the following day, he found the young lad and took him back to his abbey.

The jubilant MacNabs rowed back up the loch, their spirits high and their energy renewed with the adrenalin flowing through their veins. At the foot of the Beich Burn they landed and again lugged the boat up Glen Beich. Near the top, however, they decided that it was not worth carrying the boat back to Loch Tay that morning, so they left it at the head of the pass and took a short cut back to Killin over the slopes of Creag Gharbh. Reaching Eilean Ran, the twelve sons marched proudly into the great hall of the castle and handed the plaid-wrapped head to their old father, who unwrapped it in total silence. Turning it round to see the face he was well pleased, and exclaimed,

'The night *was* the night, and the lads *were* the lads.'

Since that infamous night the crest of the MacNab coat of arms has been the severed head of old Neish. The shield itself bears the open boat and the oars used on the moonlight raid.

Iain Min MacNab was a notable soldier in later years. He fought for the Marquis of Montrose and became his commander of the castle of Kincardine in the Mearns, although the fortress was by then in ruins, having been destroyed in 1646. He took part in, and survived, the Battle of Worcester in 1651, where he led three hundred of his clansmen against Oliver Cromwell's victorious force. He was killed two years later by Cromwellian forces, after which Eilean Ran Castle was set on fire and abandoned (General George Monck had to intervene to protect MacNab's widow and children from suffering the same fate as the chief). A contemporary account by an English commander notes the circumstances:

> The Lord MacKnab, one of the great Montrossians, with his whole clan, did rise upon our partie; and coming to them, after some little parley (we having got some of their cattel together) they offered our partie free quarter, if they would lay downe arms and return in peace. But our men, not willing to be so affronted, stood upon their defence; which the Highlanders perceiving, sent a flight of arrows and a volley of shot among them; and ours letting fly again at them, killed MacKnab, the great chieftain of that wicked clan, with four more, and fell upon them and routed them all.

The ribs of the ancient MacNab boat were still to be seen on the upper stretches of Glen Beich as late as 1895. Isabel MacDougall, whose great-uncle was the tenant of Dall, near Ardeonaig on the shores of Loch Tay, related that the ribs were visible in the severe winter of that year, and that her great-uncle had noticed much of the boat buried among the heather in 1854. It is said that a piece of timber from this boat is preserved by a Neish descendant in Canada. As further proof that it was possible to carry a boat across such rough upland countryside, a group of Black Watch territorials copied the feat in 1965, as an exercise in strength and stamina and in commemoration of the original event.

27 MacNaghten of Dundarave
The False Wedding

The lands of Dundarave lay sandwiched between two great estates of the Campbells. (When Donald MacNaghten fought with the MacDougalls against King Robert the Bruce in the fourteenth century some of the clan's lands were taken from them and granted to the Campbells.) Their castle, which is named 'fortress of the two oars' (Dun da ramh in Gaelic) is a magnificent tower house five storeys high that stood in ruins for a number of years until restored in 1911 by architect Sir Robert Lorimer for Sir Andrew Noble of Ardkinglas. The castle was built on a rock by the side of Loch Fyne, and either side are shingle shores where the chiefs could haul up their galleys. It was styled *Castle Doom* in Neil Munro's novel of that name. The tower dates from 1596 and was built to replace the older fortress of Castle Dubh Loch, which stood on an islet, or crannog, in the Dubh Loch at the foot of Glen Shira. The Dubh Loch fortress was said to date from the fourteenth century, but it was abandoned in 1560 after being visited by the black plague.

Dundarave belonged to the MacNaghtens (the name is sometimes spelled Macnaughton), who also held the Castle of Fraoch-eilean, which lies in the midst of Loch Awe, at the request of King Alexander III. According to an old account of the parish of Glenorchy:

In the year 1267 King Alexander III granted to Gilchrist MacNaughtan and his heirs the keeping of his Castle and island of Frechelan, Lochow, so that they should cause it to be built and repairit at the King's expense as often as needful, and keep it safely for the King's necessity, and that as often as he should come to it, the Castle well furnished should be delivered to him to lodge and dwell there at his pleasure.

Dundarave Castle

Alexander MacNaghten was a noted adherent of Charles I and as a result sustained many losses. At the Restoration Charles II knighted him and granted him a pension for life. Sir Alexander spent most of his later years in London, where he died in 1685, but, despite enjoying royal favour, he left to his son John an estate that was burdened by debt. John MacNaghten, 16th Chief, fought for

King James under 'Bonnie' Dundee at Killiecrankie in 1689, leading a considerable group of his clansmen. This attachment to the House of Stuart led to denunciation as a Jacobite rebel, and his lands were forfeited in 1691. Many forfeited lands, including those of MacNaghten, were restored within a few years.

The MacNaghten lands were coveted by the neighbouring Campbells – those of Inveraray to the west, those of Ardkinglas to the east – and they were eventually acquired by the Ardkinglas Campbells, not through battle but by means of a trick.

John MacNaghten of Dundarave fell in love with the beautiful Margaret, the youngest of the three daughters of Sir James Campbell of Ardkinglas. He proposed to her and was accepted, so, with some trepidation, he went to Ardkinglas Castle to seek her father's consent. He was shown in to the great hall of the tower and slowly approached the high table where the Campbell chieftain sat with his retainers around him.

'I love your daughter Margaret, and I am here to ask your permission for her hand in marriage.'

The hall went deathly silent, for the servants knew of the long-standing enmity between the two clans.

'Of course you can,' came the reply. 'I knew that my daughter was fond of you, and I am glad to allow her to marry the Chief of MacNaghten.'

John MacNaghten was astounded by the reply, and relieved that his proposal had been accepted by the old enemy. A bottle of whisky was opened, and a toast was proposed to the future bride and groom. John and his fiancée were dumbfounded by her father's willingness to accept him as a son-in-law, but enjoyed the celebrations which lasted long into the night.

A few months passed while preparations were made for the wedding (which took place around the year 1700). On the appointed day, John MacNaghten dressed himself in his finest clothing, and his family joined him for the short sail across the loch to the shore of Ardkinglas, where their galleys anchored. They were welcomed into the great hall of Ardkinglas Castle, where the Campbells were ready to greet them. The whisky was produced again, and all were invited to take a dram or two. A great feast had been prepared, and the MacNaghtens and Campbells sat down together to the roast which had been cooked in the castle kitchen. It was washed down with the finest claret that the Campbells could buy, more whisky was offered round, and when the time came for the ceremony, the MacNaghtens were rather jolly, and ready for the dancing which would follow.

A minister was brought in to the hall, and John MacNaghten stood before him with his Campbell bride who wore a long flowing dress of white lace with a heavy veil. The wedding vows were eagerly exchanged, and soon the ceremony gave way to a ceilidh which the two families greatly enjoyed – taken as a sign that their feud was now dead and buried.

The Campbell chieftain, however, had planned the whole cere-mony with precision, and part of his plan was to get the MacNaghtens drunk. Margaret the youngest daughter, who was to marry John, was taken away and locked up in a room and Jane, one of her elder sisters (who through the eyes of drink looked not unlike her), was substituted. However, in the cold sobriety of day, she was no femme fatale, and she had had no suitors throughout her years of womanhood. The newly-weds took leave of the party and went to a bedroom on an upper floor of the tower. The next morning John woke up next to the elder, ugly daughter.

He soon pieced together the happenings of the night before and realised that the chieftain had duped him. Meanwhile, though, all his family had returned to Dundarave, and he was alone in the Campbell household; the first thing to do was to escape. Managing to slip out of the bedroom without waking his legal wife, he crept along the passage and in one of Ardkinglas's three round towers found a small turret room which was locked. He broke the lock and found his 'true' bride, still bound and gagged, her face stained with tears. John quickly released her, and together they managed to make their escape from the castle.

The two of them found a ship and managed to emigrate to north-ern Ireland, where they spent the rest of their lives together. (A distant cousin, Shane Dubh MacNaghten, had settled in Antrim in 1580, and it is likely that they lived with his descendants for a time.)

Back at Ardkinglas, meanwhile, the deserted Jane lamented long and bitterly, composing a Gaelic song entitled Caoidh MhicNeachdain an Duin:

O, the night is so cold, all alone I am weeping;
While the world is asleep, lonely watch I am keeping.

It also turned out that she was pregnant, and in due course she gave birth to a son. Sir James Campbell took a deep interest in the child, and, when he was old enough, often took him fishing on the loch and by the rivers. This may have been part of a plan – for one day Sir James returned to Ardkinglas in a distressed state and through tears (which he did not usually show) told his daughter the terrible news; her son had fallen into the Kinglas Water, near the Cairndow Inn, and drowned in the raging torrent. His grief was rather short-lived, however, and it was not long before it was said behind his back that Sir James had caused the lad's death because he was the heir to Dundarave. (When he died John MacNaghten left no heir, and the chiefship of his clan passed to his Irish kinsman, Edmond, 17th Chief.)

Sir James Campbell later managed to claim the lands of Dundarave, getting them escheated on the grounds that John MacNaghten was an absconding adulterer; claiming that MacNaghten was guilty of incest, he was then able to claim the forfeited estates from the crown. The formal disposition took place in 1710. These lands were then granted to his eldest daughter, Jane, who had managed to acquire a husband in Sir James Livingstone, a son of the Earl of Callander. They adopted the surname Campbell so that they could adhere to Sir James's will and inherit Ardkinglas.

28 MacNeil of Barra
Last of the Vikings

The MacNeils of Barra lived by the sea, for their lands on Barra and surrounding islands were only accessible by boat. The clan claims to have been settled on Barra from time immemorial (when Gilleonan MacNeil's ownership of Barra was confirmed by charter in 1427 it was claimed that his father, Ruaraidh MacNeil, was the thirty-fourth Ruaraidh to hold the island). The family's ancient seat is Kisimul Castle, which stands on a tiny islet in Castle Bay at the southern end of the island. Long ruined, it was restored between 1938 and 1970 by Robert Lister MacNeil (45th chief of the clan and an American architect) and is now owned by his son, Prof. Ian R. MacNeil.

In the late sixteenth century, the 15th chief of the clan, Ruaraidh, or Roderick, terrorised the islands on the west coast of Scotland, and was described as 'last of the Vikings'. Ruaraidh succeeded his grandfather, Gilliganan MacNeil, who had been one of the members of the council of the Isles who went with Donald Dubh, Lord of the Isles, to Ireland, where they swore allegiance to the English King. Gilliganan's heir, another Ruaraidh, predeceased his father, being shot at the Battle of Glenlivet on 3 October 1594 (See Chapter 10). Ruaraidh Og, as the grandson was known, spent much of his time raiding the surrounding islands and one of his epithets was Ruaraidh 'n Tartair, 'Ruaraidh the Turbulent' – so often did he sail the seas during the better weather that he also gained the name of 'the Summer Wanderer'. He was described as a 'hereditary outlaw' and was reported to the Privy Council times without number.

Some of Ruaraidh's raids took him as far south as the Irish coast, where he plundered the lands of the O'Malleys of Connaught, causing a long-standing feud. He is reputed to have had a veritable Aladdin's cave of stolen goods stored in Kisimul, from French

Kisimul Castle, Barra

brandy to silver plate and gold jewellery – though the story that three black horses stabled on the island had shoes made from melted gold ornaments is probably apocryphal! He is said to have thought himself the greatest person in the world, and all others subordinate in rank. Each evening he sent a bugler to the battlements of the castle to play a tune informing the world that 'MacNeil of Barra had now finished his meal. The princes of the earth may dine.' According to one traditional tale, when a Spanish ship ran aground on Barra the people of the island were too scared to loot it, for fear of Spanish reprisals. MacNeil, however, told them not to worry – he and the King of Spain would adjust that between themselves.

Ships gave Barra a wide berth, for fear of being captured by the chief, who was in the habit of keeping his galley hidden in one of the island's sea-lochs until a trader appeared on the horizon. On the other hand, according to Martin Martin's *A Description of the Western Isles of Scotland* (1703), Ruaraidh had the best interests of his clan at heart. He was noted for looking after widows and widowers, pairing them off so that they could still farm their crofts, and if someone became too old and infirm to look after themself, he would take them in to his own castle. Should any one lose a milking cow through some misfortune, then the MacNeil would replace it.

MacNeil's piracy extended to passing ships from Ireland, France,

Holland and England. The English Court offered a handsome reward to anyone who could apprehend him, but no one was able to do so. On one occasion an English ship sailing off the Western Isles was boarded by Ruaraidh's pirates, who stole its valuable cargo and set the crew adrift with little food. After Queen Elizabeth I complained to King James VI of Scotland about his subject's actions James summoned the chief to appear before him in Edinburgh to answer for his actions. MacNeil, however, felt that he was beyond the Scots monarch's law, and defied the summons. The King then issued a proclamation stating that MacNeil should be extirpated, and asked Kenneth MacKenzie, as Lord of Kintail, to undertake this.

MacKenzie sent a fine galley across the Minch to Barra, where it anchored in Castle Bay. A servant was sent across to Kisimul Castle in a small boat with an invitation to the chief and all his attendants to come aboard. Suspecting no hostility, MacNeil accepted. He and his men came aboard the MacKenzie ship, where they were well plied with liquor and ate the finest meal they could ever have expected. As the night wore on the servants were gradually removed and returned by boat to Kisimul. When at last only the drunken chief remained on board, he was disarmed and tied up, and the galley weighed anchor at the dead of night to take him to Edinburgh.

MacNeil was brought before the king, who asked,

'What in the name of God are you doing harassing the ships of the Queen of England?'

'I thought I'd be doing your majesty a service by annoying the woman who murdered your mother,' was MacNeil's retort.

This crafty allusion to the murder of Mary Queen of Scots influenced the King to release MacNeil, although his lands were forfeited and given to MacKenzie. (MacKenzie subsequently gave them back to MacNeil, on condition that he paid sixty merks Scots as an annual feu duty.)

In the old Highland tradition, Ruaraidh had handfasted a woman named Maclean, by whom he had several children. The tradition was that young couples agreed to set up home together, in a trial marriage, but a year and a day later were allowed to separate if no children had been forthcoming; if there were any offspring, the handfasting was blessed by the church and the marriage legitimised. Ruaraidh seems not to have adhered to the traditional spirit of the trial marriage, for he and the woman separated, and he later married the sister of the Chief of Clanranald MacDonald, by whom he had several more children.

The Captain of Clanranald declared that the second group of children were the only legitimate ones, able to inherit MacNeil's estates. He then apprehended the elder son of the first 'marriage' on a charge of involvement in a piracy incident against a ship from Bordeaux, and the son was taken to Edinburgh, but died in prison before any trial could take place.

Angered at this treatment, the dead man's brothers secured the assistance of Maclean of Duart and captured Neil Og MacNeil, the eldest son of the 'legitimate' MacDonald marriage. Fearing that old Ruaraidh might take the side of their half-brothers, they had Neil Og fettered in irons and sent to Edinburgh to be tried for taking part in the same attack on the ship. Neil Og was acquitted and set free, but the 'illegitimate' sons of the chief were ordered to exhibit their father before the Privy Council. They refused, and consequently they were denounced as rebels. The Chief of Clanranald was delighted to be awarded a commission against them, and, as a result, he was later able to install his nephew Neil Og as Chief of the MacNeils after Ruaraidh MacNeil died, in around 1613. Neil Og, who seems to have been a far more upstanding sort of person than his father, fought on the royalist side at the Battle of Worcester in 1651.

29 Macpherson of Cluny
The Chief in Hiding

Ewen Macpherson is celebrated in clan and Jacobite history as a great soldier, and one who had to conceal himself for many years following the defeat at Culloden. He was born around 1698, the son of Lachlan Macpherson and Jean Cameron, of the Lochiel family. He married Margaret, daughter of Lord Lovat, built a new house at Cluny in Badenoch in 1743 and became 12th Chief of the Macphersons on his father's death in 1746.

Ewen had received a commission in Lord Loudoun's Regiment in 1745. He was soon to hear that Prince Charles Edward Stuart had landed on the west coast of Scotland and was preparing to raise the Jacobite standard at Glenfinnan. Macpherson duly reported to General Cope at the Ruthven Barracks, but was allowed to return to Cluny and await further orders.

Bonnie Prince Charlie led his men over the hills to Garvamore, where he arrived on 28 August 1745, and sent a group of Cameron soldiers to Cluny Castle where they captured Ewen Macpherson. The Prince took his prisoner with him on his route south, but released him at Perth after Ewen had agreed to change his allegiance and follow the Prince. Sent back to Strathspey with a commission to raise his clan for the Jacobites, Ewen Macpherson followed his new cause with great enthusiasm and raised six hundred clansmen. It is said that they were the best fighting men the Prince had, and it has been noted that whenever the chief of the Macphersons led his clan in battle, they were never on the losing side.

The Macpherson men marched south under their bratach uaine, or green standard, an enchanted relic as powerful as the MacLeod's Fairy Flag. Their marching song was:

Cha till, cha till, cha till sinn tuillidh,
Gus an crùnar an Righ cha till sinne.

[No more, no more, no more we'll return,
Until the king be crowned, we'll not return.]

At first they helped to transport artillery and provisions, sent from France, from the east-coast port of Montrose south to Edinburgh. At the Battle of Falkirk they joined the line of battle, facing English dragoons, whose leather-covered helmets contained steel reinforcement plates – Macpherson is said to have remarked, 'Devil take them, these dragoons are the hardest-headed men I've ever met. I've struck at their skulls till my arm's tired, and I haven't been able to break more than a few of them.'

Ewen Macpherson was present at the head of his men when the Prince led his army south with the intention of attacking London. However, at Derby, the Jacobites, uncertain of attracting enough English supporters to carry out their attack on London, lost heart and decided to retreat back to Scotland. On the way, at Clifton Moor in Westmorland, Cluny Macpherson and his followers distinguished themselves in a moonlight battle against a superior Hanoverian force. When the long march north ended at Culloden, where the Jacobite cause was finally laid low and the Prince had to flee the field, leaving his followers in disarray, the Macphersons did not take part in the battle for the Prince had detached them to guard the various passes in Badenoch.

With the cause soundly beaten, the Macpherson contingent had to disband and flee for safety. The defeated army, the Macphersons among them, had to make their way home by stealth, for there was a price on the heads of those whom the authorities recognised as having fought for the Jacobites, and many had to flee to the mountains for safety. In the list of wanted men, the price of £1,000 was placed next to the name of Cluny Macpherson – a phenomenal figure in the eighteenth century. Yet, despite the fact that hundreds of clansmen knew his whereabouts, none was willing to reveal it. The Hanoverian captains Hugh and George Mackay were sent to Cluny Castle with orders to set it on fire, and they undertook the job with delight, setting ablaze not only the clan seat, but also any building they thought was the property of Cluny Macpherson. Lady Macpherson, who was heavy with child at the time, had to flee the castle when the Mackays arrived. She found shelter in a building which housed a corn kiln, and there gave birth to her son and heir,

'Duncan of the Kiln', before taking the child south to Edinburgh, where they took refuge with friends.

Ewen Macpherson spent the rest of his life in hiding. The Prince joined him in his secret hide-out at Ben Vricht on 20 June 1746, along with Macpherson of Breacachy and a doctor, Sir Stewart Thriepland. The Prince had few clothes when he arrived, and three of Ewen's sisters were contacted to make him new ones. They also organised men to travel in the mountains to supply the fugitives with food and drink. After a few days the band moved on to a shieling known as 'Uiskchilra' (perhaps Culra, which is named on modern maps) but found it extremely smoky and damp.

It was decided to move further into the mountain fastness, to a spot on the slopes of Ben Alder, overlooking Loch Ericht. Known as 'Cluny's Cage', this hideaway comprised a huge boulder with a hut built of tree branches on it. A manuscript of around 1756 describes it as constructed in a thicket of holly, the branches interwoven to make the walls, with a moss-thatch roof. The upper floor served as a bedchamber, the lower as a store; at the back was a hearth for cooking and baking, and the fireplace had a small chimney which dispersed the smoke among the boulders, whose colour camouflaged it from spies. There was a spring of fresh water nearby (and this is the spot that modern maps mistakenly name as 'Cluny's Cave'). The fugitives spent some time in hiding here. They wanted for little, for it was noted that they had mutton, lamb, ham, butter and cheese for eating, and a plentiful supply of whisky; although they had only one saucepan between them, the Prince used his silver spoon for eating, and they passed their time playing at cards. The Prince stayed there until September, when word reached him that the ship that was to take him to France had arrived in Loch nan Uamh. The group started out for the west, and Cluny Macpherson and the Prince parted at Uisge nam Fichead, near Glen Roy, on the border between Badenoch and Lochaber.

Ewen still had to remain concealed, however. One of his hiding-places was only two miles from the burnt-out shell of Cluny Castle: a cave on the rock cliff of Creag Dhubh, known ever since as Uamh Chluanaidh, or Cluny's cave (the clan's war cry is Creag Dhubh Chloinn Chatain – the black rock of Clan Chattan). The cave is twenty-six feet deep and the low and narrow entrance is reached from a thin rock ledge that affords panoramic views of upper Strathspey, and the lower reaches of Glen Truim.

Another hide-out was inside Dalchully House, which stands

three miles west of Cluny at the foot of Strath Mashie. Here there survives a timber-lined secret chamber below the floor in which Ewen spent a good deal of time. It was here that he came closest to being captured, when troops under Hector Munro, a lieutenant in the 34th Regiment, arrived with instructions to search out the fugitive. Ewen disguised himself as a ghillie, and offered to hold the lieutenant's horse whilst the search was carried out. He told Munro that, even if he knew where the chief was, he would not betray him, not even for the thousand-guinea reward. Munro replied, 'I believe you would not. You are a great man. Here is a shilling for you.'

It is said that Ewen Macpherson had yet another subterranean hide-out, in the holm (the flat land beside a river) next to the Spey. His clansmen had dug it for their chief, working under cover of darkness and throwing the soil into the river, where it was washed away as silt, so as to avoid creating a tell-tale pile of freshly dug earth. A timber roof, covered with sods of turf was made, and under it Cluny hid for many a long month until the day when it gave way and a surprised stranger landed on top of him. Macpherson was about to slay him with his dirk but hesitated, and instead made him swear never to reveal his whereabouts. The stranger swore his oath and departed, but a few hours later Macpherson decided that he had taken too great a risk and changed his hiding place; soon afterwards the hole in the ground was raided, but the soldiers found it empty. At the end of the nineteenth century a piper named Sandy MacDonald was ferreting near this hide-out when one of his ferrets got stuck down a hole. While digging it out MacDonald unearthed six claymores.

In June 1755 Ewen Macpherson managed to make his way to the coast and escape to France. He probably went to report to Prince Charlie, for the Prince had written to 'C.M. in Scotld.' on 'Ye 4th September 1754' as follows:

Sir,
this is to desire you to come as soon as you can conveniently to Paris, bringing over with you all the effects whatsoever that I left in your hand when I was in Scotland, as also whatever money you can come at, for I happen to be at present in great straits, which makes me wish that you should delay as little as possible to meet me for that effect. You are to address yourself when arrived at Paris, to Mr John Waters, Banker, &c. He will direct you to where you will find your sincere friend,

C.P.

The request for money alluded to the fact that the Prince had left behind £27,000 in the careful hands of Cluny, with instructions not to spend one farthing without an order from him.

Thereafter, Cluny Macpherson lived in exile in France, where his wife followed him in 1757. However, his health was failing, and he died the following year, aged 58, at Dunkirk, where he was buried in the garden of the Carmelites. His widow returned to Scotland, where she died in April 1765 and was buried in the Cluny burial ground. Ewen Macpherson's lands had been forfeited, but were eventually restored to his son, Duncan, 13th Chief, in 1784.

30   MacQuarrie of Ulva
A Hospitable Welcome

Ulva is a rather rocky island of around six thousand acres which lies
between Loch Tuath and Loch na Keal off the western coast of Mull.
Anciently it was the home of the chief of the MacQuarrie family, a
clan belonging to Clan Alpin, which relied on the help of its larger
neighbours, the MacDonalds and Macleans. The island was sold by
the 16th Chief, Lachlan MacQuarrie, in 1778, to pay off his debts.
His cousin, also Lachlan (1761–1824), became Governor of New
South Wales in Australia, from 1809–21.

Dunslaff MacQuarrie, who succeeded his father in 1473, married
a daughter of MacNeill of Taynish, and the bride's dowry included
a piebald horse, along with two men and two women. He supported
the Macleans of Duart, and as a result gained the protection of that
greater clan. In 1504 he was summoned before the Scottish parliament as 'MacGorry of Ullowaa' to answer for his part in the rebellion of Donald Dubh, who claimed the Lordship of the Isles. In
1517 he was given a remission for his support. However, he was an
elderly man when he was involved in an incident that could have
cost him his own life and the lands of his clan. He was saved by his
quick-thinking and hospitality.

Lachlan Cattanach Maclean of Duart, tenth Chief of the
Macleans, had an affair with one of the beautiful young women of
his clan, and she bore a son who was named Allan Maclean, though
better known by his nickname of Alein nan Sop, ('Allan of the
straw'), for he was born in a barn. She then married the Maclean
who was the laird of Torloisk, an estate on the west side of Mull,
overlooking Loch Tuath. Her husband loved her, but he was jealous
of her love for her son, and whenever the lad went to see him, the
stepfather would turn his back on him and ignore him. Of the many

incidents of cruelty the one that stuck in Allan's mind was the time when he approached Torloisk, just as his mother was making some cakes for him on the fire. When Allan entered the house his stepfather grabbed one of the cakes off the griddle and forced Allan's hands around it. The heat of the cake left the boy's hands badly burned, and the palm of his hand was scarred for the rest of his life. Eventually, Allan was sent away to be brought up by Torloisk's elderly neighbour Dunslaff MacQuarrie.

Dunslaff managed to raise the lad, though not without some difficulty, for Allan was a rather reckless and disruptive child, and the old man had a good deal of trouble in keeping him under control. When he grew up, though, Allan decided to leave and become a sailor, so he joined the Danish pirate ships, which at this time were often found on Scotland's western seaboard. Before long, he found himself in charge of one; after a number of years he took command of a flotilla of ships, and his name became known along the west coast as a fearless and capable seaman. In 1530 he was responsible for killing Neill MacNeill, Chief of the MacNeills of Gigha, and a number of his clansmen in a feud. On behalf of Alan MacDonald of Islay, who had forcibly taken it from the Campbells, he took command of Tarbert Castle, overlooking Loch Fyne. This he made his base for raids into Arran, Cowal, parts of Ayrshire and even Ireland. One tale relates how he attempted to rape a daughter of the MacNeil of Barra whilst visiting the castle on Carn na Burgh Mor, but one of MacNeil's servants intervened and pushed him over a cliff. Fortunately for him, he landed on a ledge and survived; the ledge was thereafter known as Urraich Ailean na Sop, or Allan of the Straw's shelf.

One day, longing to meet his mother again, Allan Maclean returned to Mull. He sailed his ships into Kilninian Bay, anchoring in sight of Torloisk House, and as he rowed ashore he was surprised to see his stepfather running down to the beach to welcome him home – although he bore the sad news that his mother had died some months before. It turned out that Allan's surprising welcome was due to the fact that Maclean of Torloisk had a long-standing feud with the MacQuarries of Ulva, and saw in his stepson's arrival a way of exacting vengeance. He told Allan that it was time he gave up the sea and settled on some land. It would be very easy, he said, to claim the island of Ulva, for the old laird was infirm and unable to protect himself. If Allan could kill him, he would be able to stake a claim to the island.

Allan agreed to his stepfather's proposal, and his galleys sailed southward to anchor in the Sound of Ulva, which was overlooked by the chief's house. Old Dunslaff MacQuarrie was rather alarmed to see them in the bay, fearing both for his life and the safety of his clan, and he waited with trepidation as he saw Allan make his way ashore with a band of heavily armed soldiers. Dunslaff knew only too well that Allan had killed many of his wife's family in a feud in 1530 for the Taynish MacNeills were a branch of the Gigha MacNeills. He therefore decided that it would be best to greet the visitors and treat them well, in the hope that they might decide to leave again in peace.

He welcomed Allan into his house, plied him with spirits and ordered a feast to be prepared. That evening they both enjoyed the meal, spent a long time discussing the people of the islands and the events of the past years, and the older chief recalled the feuds of his younger days. As night began to fall, Allan decided that he must return to his ships, but as he left, he turned to his host and told him that he had really enjoyed the blether, but that the evening had cost him dear.

'How is that,' the chief asked, 'when I have prepared the meal and provided the entertainment at no cost to yourself?'

'That is very true,' replied Allan. 'But when I came here I planned to kill you, take possession of your castle and island, and settle myself here as the laird of Ulva. However, your hospitality has made me feel that it would be treacherous to do such a thing.'

'Those plans sound as if they were not of your own making,' replied Dunslaff. 'They sound more like those of your stepfather, the old laird of Torloisk, who has been my sworn enemy these last few years.'

He went on to tell Allan how badly Torloisk had treated his mother, and reminded him of the poor treatment he himself had received as a lad.

'Would it not be more suitable to attack an old devil who has never treated you well, rather than kill an old lad like me, who has always thought highly of you, and looked after your needs.'

Allan Maclean agreed and, recalling the scorched fingers of his youth, returned to Torloisk. His stepfather again came eagerly to meet him, expecting to hear of the death of MacQuarrie. But Maclean bounded towards him, shouting.

'You old villain. You tried to get me to murder a better man than yourself. Do you not remember how you scorched my fingers with a burning cake? Today is the day you must pay for your actions.'

He drew his sword from his belt, and slew the laird with a single blow.

Allan Maclean took possession of Torloisk estate, which remained in his family's possession for many years. He is said to have died about 1555 and was buried on Iona, where his grave-stone can still be seen at Realaig Orain. Dunslaff MacQuarrie lived on for a number of years and remained a good friend of his former ward. In later years his grandson, Hector, married a daughter of Lachlan Og Maclean of Torloisk, thus uniting the two families in friendship.

31 MacThomas of Glenshee
The Great Swordsman

Clan MacThomas (also known as MacComie or MacCombie, the pronunciation of the Gaelic, MacThomais) is one of the smallest Highland clans. It owned the lands of Thom (or Tomb, as it is marked on modern maps) and Finegand in Glenshee, Perthshire, where its members had settled after emigrating from further north in the fifteenth century. This clan was part of the greater Mackintosh clan, and thus part of Clan Chattan, and the family traced its descent from Thomas Mor, whose grandfather was William, eighth Chief of Clan Chattan.

The seventh Chief of the MacThomases, best known by his Gaelic appellation of Iain MacThomais Mor, or 'big' John MacComie, is celebrated in Perthshire legend. He was born sometime in the early seventeenth century and married an Elizabeth Campbell, a member of the Argyll clan, with whom he had seven sons. Iain Mor was notorious in the district for his hatred of tax-collectors, especially those who collected dues on behalf of the Earl of Atholl.

One day Atholl's men came into Glen Shee to collect taxes from an old widow who lived near Finegand. They rode up to the croft-house and banged their sticks loudly on the door. The frightened old woman opened the door and was presented with a demand for payments due to the Earl. She had no money to give them, so they took most of her poultry, which left her with virtually no means of supporting herself. The widow ran to Finegand as fast as her aged legs would carry her to tell MacThomas what had happened, and, incensed at her treatment, Big John gathered some of his men and set off in pursuit of the collectors. They soon caught up with the Atholl men and routed them on the spot. The poultry was all

145

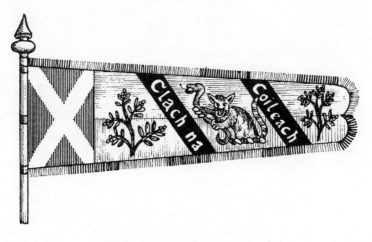

Chief of the MacThomases' pinsel

gathered up, apart from a cock which flew up on top of a large boulder, where it stood proudly, flapping its wings and crowing. Known ever since as Clach na Coileach (the Cock Stone) the boulder became the clan rallying-place. In 1968 a gate and path to the stone was erected in memory of a distant clansman, Harold Edward MacCombie of California.

The feud between the MacThomas clan and Atholl's men reached such a pitch that the Earl of Atholl sent to Italy for the services of one of that country's greatest swordsmen. Challenged to a duel, MacThomas readily agreed to meet the foreign champion, and when they met, Lord Atholl was shocked to find that Iain Mor's swordsmanship was too good for his Italian import.

In 1644 John MacThomas set off for Dundee to join the forces of James Graham, Marquis of Montrose. He went north with Montrose's army to the sack of Aberdeen by the royalist forces on 13 September, at which he captured Sir William Forbes of Craigievar, the Sheriff of Aberdeen and a commander in the covenanting army; Forbes led a charge at the royalists, and Iain Mor managed to unhorse him and take him prisoner.

When Montrose was defeated at Philiphaugh in September 1645 MacThomas returned to Glenshee and proceeded to extend the clan lands considerably along the northern edge of Strathmore, acquiring Glen Prosen (where there are a number of places associated with him: MacComie Mor's Putting Stone, MacComie Mor's Wells and

MacComie Mor's Chair) and Strathardle. He bought the Barony of Forter from the Earl of Airlie in 1652 and, as Forter Castle was in ruins, built himself a new house at Crandart, on the banks of the River Isla. Many tales are told of Iain Mor. He is said to have overcome a fierce bull with his bare hands, and it is also reputed that, suspecting that his son was not as good a fighter as he was, he disguised himself and picked a fight with his heir – after a brutal struggle MacComie Mor satisfied himself that his son was a suitable successor.

At the Restoration in 1660 the royalists, who felt that MacThomas's support had waned during the Commonwealth, took action against him, and Parliament fined him heavily for some of his actions. Around the same time the Earl of Airlie took legal action to reclaim the Forest of Caenlochan, despite the fact that he himself had sold it to MacThomas as part of the Barony of Forter. Being out of favour, MacThomas lost his case, although he continued to graze his cattle on the upper reaches of the Isla. Lord Airlie, though, having regained the charter to the lands, leased them to Iain Mor's cousin, Farquharson of Broughdearg (in Glenshee).

The resulting dispute between them led to a fight at Drumgley, just west of Forfar in Angus, on 28 January 1673. At a spot since known as MacCombie's Field the Farquharsons and MacThomases fought each other, and Farquharson of Broughdearg and two of Iain Mor's sons were killed. The feud between the two families was largely carried on in the courts, however, and the accumulating legal costs and fines left John MacThomas in severely straitened circumstances. After he died in 1676 his surviving sons were forced to sell off most of their lands.

32 Matheson of Matheson
The Siege of Eilean Donan

The Clan Matheson claim descent from Gilleoin, who is said to have been a younger son of the ancient royal family of Lorne. The name derives from the Gaelic MacMhathain, ('sons of the heroes'), and the earliest chiefs are so styled. Cormac or Kenneth MacMhathain, second chief of the clan, fought the Vikings at the important Scots victory at the Battle of Largs in 1263. Thereafter the clan supported the MacDonald Lords of the Isles and prospered until the Battle of Harlaw in 1411, where its chief Alasdair Matheson was captured. Thereafter the Lordship of the Isles was much reduced, and the Mathesons lost much of their influence and their lands, much of the latter being claimed by their neighbours to the east, the MacKenzies. By the early sixteenth century the Mathesons had switched their allegiance to the MacKenzies because of a feud with the MacDonalds of Sleat. Their chief Iain Dubh (Black John) Matheson married Isabel, the widow of Sir Dugald MacKenzie and daughter of Duncan Ban Grant of Glen Moriston, cementing the new bond between the two clans, and Iain Dubh was then appointed keeper of Eilean Donan Castle on the MacKenzie's behalf. In 1532 he entertained King James V, who was on his way to the Western Isles to demand the allegiance of the clans, and try to settle some of the feuds which were taking place.

In 1539 the MacDonalds of Sleat launched an attack on Eilean Donan in the course of a campaign by Donald Gorm, their sixth Chief, to reclaim the Lordship of the Isles which his father, Donald Gruamach, had held. With a band of 400 soldiers behind him, he sailed his fifty galleys up the Sound of Sleat, through the narrows of Kyle Rhea and into Loch Alsh. At the junction of Loch Long with Loch Duich stood Eilean Donan. Although Iain Dubh was in residence, the castle was only lightly garrisoned at the time, and the MacDonalds did not expect much resistance to their attack.

Eilean Donan Castle, before it was restored

They anchored in the bay and sent a small troop to force the castle's sea-gate, at that time the only opening in the enclosure wall. However, the small garrison defended the castle bravely. Placed high on the battlements, they had an excellent field of fire and shot arrows and crossbow bolts at the many ships anchored around the islet. As the MacDonalds attacked, an archer on the battlements of the castle aimed his arrow at the leg of the MacDonald chieftain (most of the rest of his body was covered in armour). The arrow whistled through the air, and its point found a gap in the steel and pierced its target's leg. With a gasp of pain the MacDonald wrenched it free, but, as he did so, the keen edge of the arrowhead severed an artery; the chief collapsed where he stood and quickly expired from loss of blood.

Their chief slain, the MacDonalds decided to withdraw, and amid a hail of projectiles raining down on them from the castle they managed to weigh anchor and set sail for Skye. The garrison's relief that it had successfully repelled a superior force, and that Eilean Donan remained in Mackenzie hands, was marred by the death of Iain Dubh Matheson, who had been struck down by a bolt from a MacDonald crossbowman.

Duncan MacRae, who according to some accounts was the archer whose arrow felled Donald Gorm MacDonald, became the temporary Constable of the castle in 1539. He married Iain Dubh's widow, by whom he had a son, Christopher MacRae, who also became Constable of the castle.

33 Menzies of that Ilk
The Wedding Feast

Castle Menzies, a very fine Z-plan tower house with pepper-pot turrets, carved dormer windows, and coats of arms over the door, stands in the rich countryside of the Strath of Appin across the River Tay from Aberfeldy. It was the seat of the Menzies chiefs from the sixteenth century until 1918, when the sister of Sir Neil Menzies of that Ilk died, the last of her line. In 1957 it was acquired by the Menzies Clan Society, who have undertaken considerable restoration work and returned the building to much of its glory, and today it is regularly open to the public.

Our tale concerns the wedding of Sir Alexander Menzies, the 2nd Baronet of that Ilk. When it came time for him to take a bride, he looked no further than Finlarig at the opposite end of Loch Tay, where he wooed his full cousin, Christian Campbell, the daughter of Lord Neil Campbell and grand-daughter of the Marquis of Argyll.

On 14 June 1646, as Alexander was on his way to Finlarig for the wedding feast, he met an old woman by the roadside, who revealed herself as the witch of Sron a' Chlachain. She stopped him and asked him where he was heading.

'To my wedding at Finlarig,' he said.

'I'm sorry to tell you,' she responded, 'that ere night falls there will be blood flowing into Loch Tay.'

Alexander laughed at the old wife and dismissed her tale as little more than nonsense. He went on to the wedding and, after it, to the reception, held by Lord Neil in the great hall of Finlarig, the likes of which hadn't been seen in the district for many a year. There was a fine ox roasting at the fire, the claret was flowing freely, and the company was grand. As the night wore on, the guests were having a grand time, and Alexander forgot all about the old woman.

Suddenly someone was battering furiously at the castle's oak door, his attempts to attract attention almost drowned out by the noise within. A guest went down to answer the door, admitted the stranger and invited him up to the wedding feast. When he arrived in the great hall the man announced to the guests that a party of MacDonells from Keppoch were returning with cattle from Glen Dochart, where they had raided many houses and set some on fire.

It seems that a group of MacDonells had been reiving cattle across much of the central Highlands, travelling in a loop over Rannoch Moor and Glen Dochart, and they were now returning north over the heights of Mamlorn. Apart from the fact that cattle had been stolen from Glen Dochart, the Campbells were incensed that they had not been told of the raiding party passing over their lands. In those days it was customary for raiders to give a percentage of their lifted cattle to the owners of the land over which they had passed – known as 'road collop', this custom gave rise to numerous feuds between clans.

The men in the castle were outraged, and rose from the banquet, gathered up their arms and set off in pursuit. Spotting the cattle high on the hill above Killin, they decided to head straight up the hill and catch them. Alexander, who had previous experience in the forces of the Swedish King Gustavus Adolphus, advised that it would be easier and safer to circle the hill and come on the MacDonells from above, but the Campbell hotheads were unwilling to listen and preferred to make a direct attack up the hillside. Following the trail of the cattle, they came across the thieves in a hollow in the hillside, and a battle ensued. In the melèe the effect of the alcohol they had drunk made the Campbells' aim less steady and dulled their reflexes and the reivers managed to escape. When they eventually pulled back, the wedding party counted its losses: 40 dead, and 21 badly injured. Alexander Menzies was relatively lightly wounded – he had received nine arrow gashes to his legs and thighs – and, as he sat on the hillside contemplating the débâcle, he noticed the blood-red waters of the little burn which issued from the corrie. His eye followed the waters down the hillside into the loch, and he remembered the old woman's prophecy. From that day to this the stream has been known as Allt Fuileach, or the Bloody Burn.

A rider galloped the length of Loch Tay to bring word of the events to the other Campbell seat of Balloch Castle, and mounted reinforcements came quickly back along the lochside and set off after the MacDonells. They rode west up Glen Lochay and came upon the raiders at Coire nam Bannoch, on the slopes above Glen Orchy. The Campbells' superior numbers, and the fact that they were fresh, whereas the MacDonells had had to fight for their lives once already, meant that the encounter was a short one, and nearly all the raiders were killed, including Alasdair, the son of the clan chief. (It was said that Alexander Menzies was responsible for the young MacDonell's death, cutting off his head with one great swipe of his claymore). Afterwards the cattle were gathered together and driven back down to Glen Dochart, and Alexander Menzies returned to his new bride to begin their many happy years of married life.

34 Munro of Foulis
Witches and Wizardry

The Munros, whose name is thought to derive from 'mountaineers of Ross', were originally vassals of the Earls of Ross, although when the earldom was forfeited in 1476 they held their lands from the Crown. These lands were on the north side of the Cromarty Firth, and occupied the two parishes of Kiltearn and Alness. The clan seat is still at Foulis Castle, where the present chief farms around 1,300 acres of prime countryside.

Back in the sixteenth century the 17th chief of the clan was Hector Munro of Foulis, (c1540–1603). He was the second surviving son of Robert Mor Munro (who died in 1588) and his first wife Margaret Ogilvie. Before he succeeded his elder brother Robert (who outlived their father by only eight months) Hector had studied for the church, as many second sons did, and Queen Mary commissioned him as Chaplain of Newmore and later of Obsdale. He was appointed Dean of Ross in the Protestant church, against the opposition of the previous dean, Alexander Urquhart, and kept this office until he succeeded as clan chief.

Hector's father made a second marriage to Lady Katherine Ross, daughter of the ninth Chief of Ross of Balnagown. It is not clear whether she influenced her stepson or not, but both she and Hector became involved in the occult. Lady Katherine's brother, George Ross, had married a second wife, Marjorie Campbell, and Hector and Lady Katherine sought the death of both her and Hector's brother Robert. This would enable George Ross to marry Robert Munro's widow and in due course would allow Hector to succeed as chief of the Munros, the process linking the Ross and Munro families even more closely.

To carry out their plan, Hector and Lady Katherine employed

the witches of Tain, two of whom, Marion (or Marjorie) MacAllister and William MacGillivray, gave their advice and assistance. Marion, who was known in Gaelic as Loisg na Lodar, or 'burn the ladle', made a clay model of Lady Marjorie and told Lady Katherine that she should shoot tiny 'elf arrows' at the effigy; this would cause the real Marjorie to suffer injury and die. The wizard MacGillivray suggested quicker methods: he supplied the pair with a poison, known simply as 'witchcraft', which in fact was probably nothing more than rat poison, bought from a trader in Elgin. However, Hector and Lady Katherine either failed to carry out their instructions properly, or else the potions were not strong enough. Although she did become a bed-ridden invalid, Marjorie did not die, and survived for a further 13 years (a servant who had tasted the potion died within minutes, though). Whether any attempt was made on Robert Munro's life is unknown.

After the word was out that she was involved in the attempted murders, Lady Katherine fled to Caithness and remained there for almost a year. Nonetheless, Hector and his step-mother were tried at the Justice Court held in Fortrose Cathedral on 28 November 1577, along with MacGillivray and MacAllister, who told the aghast jury the whole story. Apparently MacAllister and Christina Ross Malcolmson had helped to make the clay models, the wizard John MacMillan had sold them special arrowheads for four shillings, and the witch Agnes Roy had spoken to the fairies on Lady Katherine's behalf. MacGillivray was condemned to be burnt at the stake, as was Christina Ross (MacAllister seems to have avoided death, perhaps because her methods required no physical contact or poison, although she was probably imprisoned for a time). The laird's wife and son were acquitted, however - perhaps because they were local landowners, and the jury feared for their tenancies and jobs.

A number of years later, in 1589, Hector Munro was taken ill. (By this time he was laird of Foulis Castle and chief of the clan, his brother having died - by fair means or foul). He was in such pain that he feared death was imminent, and he resorted to witchcraft to prevent it. He sent one of his retainers to see a local cailleach, or witch, and bring her back with him to Foulis Castle. Hector invited the witch, Marian MacIngarrath (who may be the same person as Marion MacAllister) into his private room, and dismissed the servant.

'I fear I am about to die,' he told her. 'Is there any potion or spell that you could cast over me so that I may live awhile yet, and die at a ripe old age?'

The witch looked him up and down. After a short while she told him that she knew of only one way to prevent him dying. She could not prevent death, but she was able to transfer it to someone else. If Hector followed her instructions, the grim reaper would be unable to claim his life, but would take the appointed person instead. The pair consulted for a long time and eventually decided on a plan. Hector would carry out the witch's instructions, and, instead of Hector, his half-brother, George Munro of Obsdale, would die instead. (Marian also consulted Hector's step-mother about which of the two men she would prefer to die; it is said that Lady Katherine in turn consulted the Devil himself before deciding – in the process running a distance of 'nine riggs', which must have been about a mile long. On her return she told the witch Hector was to live, and George was to die.)

One dark January night, therefore, Witch Marian returned to Foulis Castle, where the chief was waiting for her. They went to a wood a short distance away, at a mystical spot on the boundary between two baronies. There Marian, being the fitter of the two, dug a grave in the frost-hardened ground. When the grave was ready, Hector lay down in it on a blanket. Over the top Marian spread a raft of withies, or willow branches, over which she laid a thin layer of turf, and thus the makeshift grave was complete.

Within a few weeks Hector's health mysteriously improved – to the astonishment of folk in the area, who, like Hector himself, had reckoned that he was not long for this world. But, as Hector recovered, his half-brother George began to fail. He died a few months later, in 1590. Local people began to suspect that some form of witchcraft was involved, especially when it became known that a Munro servant had been sent to fetch the local witch and take her back to the laird. Hector and Katherine Munro were summoned before the court by the King's advocate, David MacGill, and on 22 June 1590 were charged with 'witchcraft, incantation, sorcery and poisoning'. They were let off, for lack of evidence, but Marian MacIngarrath was also tried, and the jury found her guilty of various offences (she seems to have confessed to her sorcery under torture). She was tied to a large stake hammered into the ground and garotted, after which her body was daubed with tar and set alight.

In 1590 an Act of Scots Parliament required Hector Munro to produce a caution of 10,000 merks security for himself and the good behaviour of his clansmen, even those living distant from Foulis on other clan lands. He seems to have settled down thereafter, and within a few months he was granted a commission by the king to apprehend the Earls of Angus, Errol, and Huntly, and a number of other gentlemen, for their part in the assassination of the Regent of Scotland, the Earl of Moray, in 1570, twenty years before.

Hector seems to have felt a need for a lawyer, for in 1591 it is recorded that he granted the farm of Teachatt in feu to one John Munro, Writer [solicitor], in payment of an annual fee as well as 'his honest personal service in all causes and legal actions' as required by the laird or his successors. However, the choice seems to have been a rather poor one for when John Munro died in 1613 he was intestate.

35 Ogilvy of Airlie
The Bonnie Hoose

Airlie Castle in Angus has been the seat of the Ogilvy family since the fifteenth century. Before then the clan occupied the lands of Glen Ogilvy in the parish of Glamis, which were given to the family around 1163 by King William the Lion. The chiefs were created Earls of Airlie in 1639 by Charles I. The Ogilvys had been involved in numerous feuds over the years. In 1526 the Mackintoshes invaded the Ogilvy lands and massacred two dozen of the gentlemen of the clan. In 1591 the Campbells attacked the Ogilvys whilst they were living peaceably in Glen Isla, killing some of the clan and causing the chief and his lady to flee for their lives.

Lord James Ogilvy, who became the second Earl, was born at Airlie Castle sometime between 1611 and 1615. He and his two brothers were educated by a tutor at St Andrews University, where their cousin James Graham, later the Marquis of Montrose, was also studying. James Ogilvy and James Graham were close friends, despite the latter's success in wooing Lady Magdalen Carnegie, whom they both had their eye on. Ogilvy married a distant cousin, Helen Ogilvy, eldest daughter of the first Lord Banff, by whom he had two sons and five daughters.

Lord James and his father were both staunch royalists. It was while his father was away at York, meeting King Charles I, that the Campbells took advantage of his absence to carry out one of their most evil crimes. The Marquis of Argyll, commander of the covenant forces, led 5,000 men into Angus in July 1640 and attacked Airlie Castle, destroying much of the building. (The castle's defence seems not to have been very spirited, and Lord James is said to have fled in the opposite direction on hearing of Argyll's approach.) It is said that the Marquis of Argyll himself took part in the castle's destruction, 'taking the hammer in his own hand and knocked down the hewed work of the doors and windows till he did sweat for heat at his work,' according to the Rev. Dr William Marshall's *Historic Scenes in Forfarshire*, written in 1860. The incident is recounted in the old ballad, *The Bonnie Hoose of Airlie*:

> The Lady looked ower her window sae hie,
> An' O, but she grat sairly,
> To see Argyll an' a' his men,
> Come to plunder the bonnie hoose o' Airlie.

The ballad is incorrect in stating that Lady Ogilvy was present at the destruction of Airlie, for it is known that she was living at the time in Forter Castle in Glen Isla. Argyll ordered an attack on this too, dispatching Dougal Campbell of Inverawe to 'demolish my Lord Ogilvy's house of Forther ... cast off the irone yettis and windows, and tak doon the roof'. In the attack Lady Ogilvy was treated cruelly; even though she was pregnant at the time, the Marquis refused to let her go and stay with her grandmother, Lady Drimmie, who was also a relative of his. Instead she made her way to Dundee where she gave birth to a daughter.

Argyll then sent a sergeant to destroy the House of Craig, also in Glen Isla, which was the home of Sir John Ogilvy. When he arrived the sergeant found that there were only a few women in the house – a sick, elderly lady and a few servants – so he left them alone and returned to the Marquis telling him that it was only an undefended building and not worth destroying. The Marquis was angry at this and ordered the sergeant to return to Craig and demolish it. All in all, the Campbells caused £7,000 worth of damage to the Airlie lands, and so despoiled them that the Earl could not take a rent for the next fourteen months.

In February 1643 Lord James joined Montrose and became his aide-de-camp, as a result of which he was charged with treason in July that year. In the winter of 1644–5 he was involved in a revenge attack on the Campbells, when Montrose led the royalists into Argyll. The Ogilvys are also said to have joined the MacLeans in setting fire to Castle Campbell in Clackmannanshire – although excavations there have revealed no evidence of this incident – and to have destroyed a number of houses in and around Dollar, the town at the foot of the castle glen. Lord James was captured in 1644 when Montrose's forces were harrying towns in the north of England; sent

Forter Castle, Glen Isla, shown restored

south with a message for the king, he was captured along with
Montrose's half-brother Harry and some others. Ogilvy remained
in gaol in Edinburgh Tolbooth until after the Battle of Kilsyth in
August 1645, when he was freed by the Master of Napier, one of
Montrose's supporters.

At the Battle of Philiphaugh, which took place in the Borders on
13 September 1645, the covenanters under General David Leslie
surprised Montrose, and Lord James begged him to make his escape,
as he was the only person who was capable of rallying the King's
supporters. Montrose did escape, but the covenanters won the day,
and James Ogilvy was again captured and imprisoned. He refused to
give up hope, reminding his captors that he and his fellow prisoners
had surrendered on condition that their lives were spared. Found
guilty for his part in the Battle of Philiphaugh at his trial on 26
November he was locked up in St Andrews Castle to await execution. The castle had only recently been brought back into use as a
prison. On 3 December a petition was sent to the authorities 'by the
prissoniers now processed, and in the castell of St Andrewes desy-
ring that they may be proceidit against, not by a committee, but that
they may be judged either by their peers, the Justice-General, or
before the whole of Parliament'. A number of notables from all over
Scotland spoke on the prisoners' behalf, including Lord Lindsay,

President of the Estates of Parliament, and the General Assembly of the Church of Scotland. However, there were rumours that Lord James's father the Earl of Airlie was mounting a rescue campaign and was about to attack St Andrews. Two hundred extra soldiers were sent to guard the castle and the prisoners received their sentences: all were to be executed, rather than receiving life sentences, as had been hoped.

On Monday 19 January 1646, the evening before the planned execution, Lord James' mother, his wife and his elder sister, Margaret Urquhart, arrived at the castle drawbridge and asked the guards to allow them to pay James (who was showing signs of serious illness) one final visit. The guards were unwilling to do so, but after the visitors had sobbed uncontrollably for some time, pleading that they might never otherwise see their relative alive again, they decided to let them in. The three ladies were taken across the castle courtyard and the heavy door was opened to let them enter the cell. The guards, by now a little more sympathetic to the grieving women, decided to leave them alone with the condemned man. When they returned later to let the women out, one of them was still crying into her handkerchief, and the other two were supporting her on either side. The men laughed to themselves at the thought of Lord James hanging from the gibbet, and as they let the women out onto the drawbridge they made fun of their grief.

Later that evening the guards went to the cell to feed their prisoners. When they opened the door they were astounded to discover that it was not Lord James who was inside, but a woman dressed in his clothes. Margaret Urquhart and James had swapped their clothes and he had escaped. A proclamation was issued offering a reward of £1,000 (sterling) for the capture of James Ogilvy 'dead or alive', but no-one betrayed him. Margaret was kept in prison for two days while the authorities decided how to punish her, but after some persuasion from people in high places she was allowed to go free – the remaining prisoners were executed in haste at the appointed time, though, for fear of any more escapes. Three years later, on 7 June 1649, an Act of Parliament was issued granting Lord James a pardon.

He soon joined the court of King Charles II at Scone in 1650. Once again, though, he was captured by Oliver Cromwell's troops, at Alyth. He was taken south to London and held prisoner in the Tower until January 1657, when he was given a short period of freedom. At the Restoration Charles II granted him a pension, though this seems to have been paid only irregularly. In 1666 he succeeded to his father's title as the Earl of Airlie, and in 1668, four years after the death of his first wife, he married Marie, the dowager Marchioness of Huntly (she was a Catholic, and so excommunicated, which led to considerable difficulty in arranging the marriage). Airlie went on to become the commander of a troop of horse, and later was appointed a Privy Councillor. He also declared his support for William of Orange, but was fined £1,200 Scots for not attending Parliament – he must have appealed against this, for in 1693 he was granted leave not to attend Parliament due to his age (which was then over 80). He eventually died in 1703, at the ripe old age of around ninety. A portrait of him by William Dobson survives.

36 Robertson of Struan
Three Jacobite Risings

Alexander Robertson of Struan, 13th Chief of Clan Donnachaidh, was perhaps the only clan chief to take part in three Jacobite Risings – those of 1689, 1715 and 1745. He was born about 1670, the second son of Alexander Robertson (he had a half-brother, Robert, by his father's first marriage). As the second son he was not expected to become the chief, so he studied for the Church at St Andrews university. However, in 1688 his half-brother died, followed a few weeks later by his father, and Alexander succeeded to the title after all.

Within a few months John Graham of Claverhouse, better known as Bonnie Dundee, launched the first Jacobite rising, against William III, and the young chief rallied his clan to follow him. His widowed mother was unhappy at this and tried to persuade her brother-in-law to prevent Alexander from joining Dundee; she wrote from Carie in May 1689, 'For Christ's sake, come in all haste and stop him, for he will not be advised by me ... he is going to Badenoch just now.' With 600 men behind him, Alexander did indeed set out to join the rebels, but Viscount Dundee was slain on the battlefield at Killiecrankie the day before the Robertsons arrived. Young Robertson and a Menzies chieftain then led their men down Strath Tay towards Perth, but General Mackay's forces repelled them, and they were forced to disperse among the hills. Having thus shown where his allegiance lay, Robertson became a wanted man, and, although he was officially below the age of majority, he was attainted in 1690 and his estates forfeited. He fled to St Germain in France, where the exiled royal family were based, and subsequently enlisted in the French army, taking part in various campaigns on the continent. After thirteen years abroad he was

granted a remission at the accession of Queen Anne and was allowed
to return to Scotland, which he did in 1703. His estates, however,
were not formally restored to him.

Peace had returned to Scotland, and Robertson made many
improvements to his lands. On a knoll overlooking the River
Tummel he built a new mansion or castle which he named The
Hermitage. The name was apt, for Robertson was a noted misogy-
nist, and would not even allow female servants within his house. On
the walls of the mansion were verses he had composed himself, often
showing an anti-feminist slant:

> In this small spot whole paradise you'll see,
> With all its plants but the forbidden tree;
> Here every sort of animal you'll find
> Subdu'd, but woman who betray'd mankind;
> All kinds of insects, too, their shelter take
> Within these happy groves, except the snake;
> In fine, there's nothing pois'nous here inclos'd,
> But all is pure as Heav'n it first dispos'd,
> Woods, hills, and dales, with milk and corns abound,
> Traveller, pull off thy shoes – 'tis holy ground.

It is said that, such was his love for nature, no animal was ever killed
in the grounds of The Hermitage whilst Robertson lived there.

Still a Jacobite at heart, Alexander would never sign any document that might imply adherence to the house of Hanover; the
Duke of Perth, in a letter of 1705, noted that he was 'ever scrupu-
lously loyal [to the Stuarts] and since his return would never take
any oath nor meddle with those who now govern'. It was not
surprising, therefore, that in 1715, when the short-lived second
Jacobite rebellion started with the Earl of Mar raising his standard at
Braemar on behalf of the Old Pretender, Robertson again decided to
follow the cause. He and 500 clansmen fought at the Battle of
Sheriffmuir – where, it is said, he ran after retreating Hanoverian
dragoons, waving his purse in the air and shouting, 'Turn round,
turn round! Fight with me for the money, if not the honour.' In the
defeat of Sheriffmuir Robertson was captured, but he managed to
escape with the assistance of a kinsman, Robertson of Invervack. A
party of Hanoverian soldiers then recaptured him, but as he was
being taken south to Edinburgh, his sister Margaret helped him to
make a second escape. Once more he had to flee the country, and

back in France he joined the Scots Brigade, in which he rose to the rank of Colonel. In 1723 his sister was able to claim the estate of Strowan (Struan) under a charter of the Great Seal, and she looked after it until his return in 1726 (she died, unmarried, in 1727). In 1731 Alexander received a remission from the British Government and was able to reclaim the estates.

It was at the time of the 'Fifteen' that Robertson looked at the clan talisman, the Clach na Brataich ('stone of the standard') – a semi-precious stone which had been in the possession of Robertson chiefs since the Battle of Bannockburn when it was found stuck to the base of the clan standard. Looking into the stone, it was said that one could foretell the future by the colour to be seen within it. When this chief looked at it he was shocked to see that a crack had appeared in it – not a positive omen.

Robertson's Jacobite persuasions remained, however, as is shown in a letter of 1730 to the minister of Kenmore in Perthshire. Robertson owned the lands of Fearnan, on the north side of Loch Tay, and some of his tenants had complained that others were sitting in their pews, and that they had to stand in the aisle as a result. Robertson wrote to the minister, Rev. John Hamilton, who seems to have had Hanoverian leanings:

Sir,
Since my tenants, I do not know by what Inspiration, are willing to hear a person of your persuasion, I hope you will not see them dispossessed. Their seats in the Kirk are well known, pray Let them sit easy and have Elbow room, Least a dispossession may Cause a Rupture amongst you, not for the Honour and Interest of that Unity, we ought to be visited in the People of God. You, who are a kind of Exorcist, cast out the Spirit of Oppression, hatred and malice, from amongst us, That every Man may possess his Paternal Inheritance, from the Throne in Westminster Abbey to the Cobbler's sate in the Kirk of Kenmore. In doing this you will be Rever'd by, Sir,
Your most hmble servt.
Alexr. Robertson, of Strowan.

The arrival of Bonnie Prince Charlie in 1745 was the closest the Jacobite cause came to succeeding. When the Prince reached Perth, Robertson (by this time 75 years old) felt that he must go and follow him. With many of his clansmen behind him, he went to Perth and presented himself before the Young Pretender, who was so overcome with emotion that he wept as he embraced him. Robertson joined the Prince's army as it marched south to Prestonpans, but it was obvious that he was too old and infirm to be of any use to them, so they decided to send him back to his homeland. After the rout at Prestonpans, they had come across the Hanoverian general Sir John Cope's carriage and belongings. Struan Robertson was dressed up in Sir John's fur-lined coat and his chain, and sent back to Rannoch in the coach. In the middle of the eighteenth century the coach road did not go as far as The Hermitage, the final few miles being muddy tracks, but after Sir John Cope's carriage had been driven as far as possible, Robertson clansmen manhandled it over the fields to The Hermitage, where it remained for many years thereafter.

Although Alexander had been of little active help to the third Jacobite rising, he was denounced a rebel and his estates forfeited once more. Hanoverian soldiers burned The Hermitage to the ground, along with other homes which belonged to him. One of these was Carie, on the southern shore of Loch Rannoch. Alexander had this house rebuilt and he lived there until his death in 1749 – uncomfortably, for the house was not panelled or plastered, and the rain regularly poured through the thatched roof. He was buried at the Robertson burial site near Dunalastair, with 2,000 clansmen and neighbours present at his funeral.

Throughout his life Alexander Robertson wrote many poems, some of which were popular at the time. These were collected into book form after his death as *Poems on Various Subjects and Occasions by the Honourable Alexander Robertson of Struan, Esq.*, and a second edition, with an additional *History and Martial Achievements of the Robertsons of Strowan* incorporated, was printed in 1785. It is said that the Baron of Bradwardine in Sir Walter Scott's *Waverley* is based on Robertson.

37   Ross of Balnagown
The Unruly Chief

The lands on the east side of the north-west Highlands, between the Cromarty and Dornoch firths, was the homeland of Clan Ross – whose name derives from the Gaelic *ros*, or promontory, denoting the large area of fertile ground projecting from Tain and Nigg out to Tarbat Ness. The name Ross was afterwards applied to the county, which was later joined to the county of Cromarty. In the fourteenth century the chiefship of Clan Ross passed to the Ross family of Balnagown Castle, a fine building that still survives eight miles north east of Alness.

One of the sixteenth-century chiefs was Alexander Ross, who succeeded as 14th Chief at an early age, when his father was killed at Tain in 1528. By his first wife, a daughter of the third Earl of Caithness, he had two children: George, his heir, and Katherine, who married Robert Munro, 15th Chief of the Munros of Foulis (and, whose involvement with witchcraft was traced in Chapter 34).

Alexander was noted for his strong will and single-mindedness, fearing neither God, King nor Government. He was responsible for terrorising many of his neighbours, robbing and pillaging their lands and destroying the homes of those who failed to supply him with sufficient booty or protection money. Many complaints were sent to the Privy Council about him, but no effective action was taken. In 1569, Ross's neighbouring tenants failed to pay their taxes, having been 'herreit and wrakkit' by him.

The members of Clan Ross were unhappy at his leadership, fearing that his recklessness might lead to his dispossession, and so too the breaking up of the clan homelands. In 1577 a group of Ross chieftains had a petition drawn up, which they all signed, exhorting Alexander to serve God, obey the laws of the Regent, James

Douglas, fourth Earl of Morton, and search for a solution to Alexander's machinations which were at that time troubling Easter Ross. Among the signatories were Alexander's son and heir, George, and the heads of the Ross cadet branches of Balmuchie, Shandwick and Tollie. The petition requested a meeting in order to settle some disputes, lest Alexander 'perish his hous, kyn and freinds and tyne [forfeit] the riggis [fields] that his fathers wan.' However, Alexander refused to be influenced by the petition, and continued to act on his own whim.

The Commendator of the Abbey of Fearn (which survives as Fearn parish church), who had received numerous complaints from his parishioners and who could not collect his rents because tenants were frightened into paying them to Ross, wrote to the King and Council to tell them 'quhat barbarous cruelties, injuries, and intollerable oppressions and bluidiched the saidis Alexander Ross committed.' A warrant was issued, and Alexander was arrested and taken south to Tantallon Castle in Berwickshire where he was held for some time before being released. Things still did not improve thereafter, and letters of fire and sword were issued against him in 1583 – his son George being one of the notable men of the area who were asked to pursue him. However, Alexander Ross evaded all further attempts at capturing him and seems to have died naturally in 1592, when George succeeded to the estate.

38   Shaw of Rothiemurchus
Battle of the North Inch

The Clan Shaw are part of the Clan Chattan confederation and trace their origins back to the same Shaw MacDuff who was the progenitor of the Mackintoshes. Shaw MacWilliam MacDuff, the fourth Mackintosh chief, acquired the lands of Rothiemurchus in 1236, and his great-grandson, Iain – second son of Angus Mackintosh, sixth chief of that clan – inherited them and became the first chief of the Shaws (although the clan also used the name Mackintosh until 1620).

Iain's son and successor as Chief, Shaw MacGillichrist Mhic Iain, was brought up at his cousin's home of Moy, seat of the Mackintosh chiefs. He had rather protruding teeth, and as a result was known in Strathspey as Sgorfhiaclach (Gaelic for 'buck-tooth').

In the fourteenth century there was considerable unrest in the central Highlands between Clan Chattan and the Camerons of Lochaber. Separate and conflicting charters to the lands of Locharkaig and Glenloy had been granted simultaneously by Robert the Bruce and the Lord of the Isles to their followers, and this set the two clans at loggerheads with each other for decades. In 1370 a band of 400 Camerons under Charles MacGillonie (or Cameron) of Strone and Invermallie made a raid into Badenoch destroying homes and stealing cattle.

On their way home they were met at Invernahavon (near Newtonmore) by an army of Clan Chattan soldiers. Before battle was joined the Mackintosh chief of Clan Chattan was approached by the chiefs of the MacPhersons and the Davidsons to settle a dispute between them over who was to lead the right wing of the army. Mackintosh gave the honour to the Davidsons, at which the MacPhersons took umbrage and withdrew their support from the confederation. The Clan Chattan men, now outnumbered by the

169

Camerons, were then soundly defeated, and the Davidson chief and seven of his sons were slaughtered, virtually wiping out this clan. At this point the MacPhersons had a change of heart, decided that they should have supported their kin, and attacked the Camerons. The latter, exhausted from the previous battle, were easily beaten.

In 1391 Shaw MacGillichrist Mhic Iain (aka Shaw Mor) was chosen to lead Clan Chattan in a raid by the Wolf of Badenoch (Alexander Stewart, Earl of Buchan, the fourth son of Robert II) which took him as far as Angus. On the way they burned Elgin Cathedral in retribution for the Bishop of Moray's censure of the Wolf for deserting his wife.

The disruption in the central Highlands was of grave concern to King Robert III, and he appealed to his friend Sir David Lindsay of Glenesk to find a solution. Lindsay was a celebrated knight, steeped in the traditions of chivalry, and was also respected by the chiefs of Cameron and Clan Chattan. He persuaded them both to take part in a trial by combat: 30 men from each clan were to fight to the death in front of an assembled audience, and the winning side would become the victor in the long-standing feud between the two clans. The combat was scheduled to take place on 28 September 1396 on the North Inch at Perth, at that time Scotland's chief city. Grandstands for the spectators were erected (at a cost of £14 2s 11d), and invitations were sent out to the principal lairds of the country; King Robert III was present, as were the Dauphin of France and the Governor of Scotland.

The chief of the Mackintoshes, an elderly man by now, was unable to lead the Clan Chattan team, and his son was not of a martial bent, so another leader had to be found. Sgorfhiaclach was chosen at the strongest among the Clan Chattan leaders, and he was appointed to select thirty of the best clansmen. The Camerons (the oldest account of the battle, Andrew of Wyntoun's *The Orygynale Cronikil of Scotland*, written in 1420, refers to 'Clahynnhe Quhewyl', and some claim the opponents were the Davidsons of Invernahavon), likewise selected thirty of their finest men, and both sides made their way to Perth.

As the clansmen marched from the centre of Perth to the North Inch, one of the soldiers of Clan Chattan took fright and ran away; he swam across the Tay and disappeared. King Robert called a halt to the proceedings, for under the laws of chivalry the fight was now invalid because the numbers were unequal. The proceedings were delayed until a new Clan Chattan volunteer could be found.

Surprisingly, one man came forward, described in old accounts as Gobha-chruim, or the crooked blacksmith. He offered to take the deserter's place on payment of one merk (another account says forty shillings) and the promise, should he survive, of maintenance for the rest of his life. With the smith making Clan Chattan's numbers back up to thirty, the combat could commence.

As the warriors marched through the streets of Perth a piper played in front. According to a MacPherson tradition it was their piper who led Clan Chattan to the North Inch, playing the Feadan Dubh, or black chanter, of the clan (which, according to legend, had fallen from heaven, playing as it fell – unfortunately it was chipped when it hit the ground, but it was nonetheless revered by the clan for centuries thereafter).

Each clansman was armed with a claymore, a dirk, an axe and a bow with three arrows. No armour was allowed in trial by combat, and the men also had to fight without their plaids. Gobha-chruim is said to have fired the first arrow (which scored a direct hit) and the trial began. In the bloody process which followed heads were severed by axes, every blow of a sword or dirk which struck an opponent drew blood, and arrows protruded from bleeding wounds. Each clansman fought with all his might to prove that right, and victory, belonged to his clan, but the battle did not last for long. At the end, eleven members of Clan Chattan were still alive, whilst only one Cameron survived – he is said to have escaped across the Tay like the man who had fled before the contest began. Of the surviving Clan Chattan members, Gobha-chruim was one, Shaw Mor another. The latter was granted as his reward the lands of Rothiemurchus, which his family had previously held from the Mackintosh chiefs. The former established a family of Smith in Strathspey – a sept of Clan Chattan known as Sliochd a' Ghobha Chruim, the race of the crooked smith.

Buck-toothed Shaw died about 1405, to be succeeded by his son James (his third son, Fearchar, was the founder of the lineage of Farquharson of Inverey). He was laid to rest in the churchyard of Rothiemurchus and a memorial raised over his grave; this has been replaced on a number of occasions, but the present memorial reads:

THE GRAVE OF SEATH MOR SGORFHIACLACH
VICTOR IN THE COMBAT AT PERTH 1396

In front of the memorial, lying on the slab, are five loaf-shaped stones. Tradition says that these came from an ancient burial mound

THE GRAVE OF
SEATH MOR
SCORFHIAGLACH
VICTOR IN THE
COMBAT AT PERTH
1396

Grave of Shaw Mor, Rothiemurchus

at the Doune of Rothiemurchus, and according to an old legend, the
Bodach an Duin, or goblin of Doune, placed a curse on the stones,
under which evil would befall anyone who removed them. Robert
Scroggie, a footman in the employment of the Duke of Bedford, is

said to have taken one of them and thrown it into the river; the Duke ordered him to return it, which he did, but three days later Scroggie drowned as he crossed the River Spey. Unfortunately, though, someone did remove the stones in 1985, and they have never been recovered. Today there are five new stones on the grave of the hero of the North Inch.

39 Sinclair of Caithness
The Wicked Earls

The Sinclair family, which claims descent from the Saint-Clair family of Normandy, at first settled at Roslin in Midlothian, where a branch remains to this day. It was the marriage of Sir Henry St Clair to the heiress of the Earl of Stratherne, Caithness and Orkney that brought it the northern lands with which it is more commonly associated. Sir Henry conquered the Faroe Islands in 1391 and explored Greenland, and it is also claimed that he sailed as far as North America, landing in what became Nova Scotia and Massachusetts long before Columbus was born. In 1455 William Sinclair was created Earl of Caithness, and it was around this time that the northern branch of the family adopted that spelling.

The Sinclairs were long a warlike clan, for, through marriage, they had Viking blood in them. George Sinclair, fourth Earl of Caithness, was a noted warmonger, described in William Anderson's *The Scottish Nation* (1859–63) as 'a cruel and avaricious nobleman, who scrupled not at the commission of the greatest crimes for the attainment of his purposes'. He succeeded as the earl and clan chief in 1529, when his grandfather was killed trying to claim his right to the Orkney Islands, and in 1545 resigned his earldom of Caithness to James V, who granted a new charter in favour of George's eldest son, John, Master of Caithness, with remainder to his heirs male and assigns.

When the Bishop of Caithness was banished to England, George Sinclair and his friend Donald MacKay of Reay laid claim to the bishop's lands, and collected rent from the tenants (they claimed to be collecting it on the bishop's behalf, but he was never to receive a penny of it). Mackay also appropriated the bishop's residence of Skibo Castle, and Sinclair his other castle of Strabister. When the

Bishop was later restored to office, both Mackay and Sinclair refused to give up the castles, and they were summoned to the court at Helmsdale, where the Lieutenant-General for northern Scotland (the Earl of Huntly) and the Earl of Sutherland were to question them. Mackay refused to attend, and was subsequently arrested and held prisoner in the Munros' castle of Foulis until his escape in 1549, but George Sinclair seems to have acted out of character, for not only did he go to Helmsdale, he risked life and limb to do so. The Helmsdale River was in full spate, but Sinclair forced his way across on foot against water that came as high as his chest. His attendance meant that he was able to come to an arrangement with the two earls, and he was free to return to Caithness.

In July 1555 Mary Queen of Scots came to Inverness to try to establish order among the northern clans. George Sinclair was commanded to appear before her, along with many of his clansmen, in order to swear loyalty to her. Sinclair went alone and, for failing to bring his men with him, was imprisoned as a possible nuisance at Inverness. He was later transferred to Aberdeen, then Edinburgh, before finally being freed on payment of a large fine. On 15 December 1556 he was granted a remission for his 'crime'.

In 1566 Sinclair became justiciar of Caithness, which gave him the power to condemn or pardon any crime committed in that county, apart from treason, and in 1567 he was the Chancellor of the jury that tried the Earl of Bothwell and acquitted him of murdering Lord Darnley. (It is worth noting that Bothwell's sister, Lady Jean Hepburn, was Sinclair's daughter-in-law!). Between 1566, when he acquired the Barony of Mey from the Bishop of Caithness, and 1572 George built the Castle of Mey – four storeys high and virtually square in plan, with a flat roof and bartizans at the corners. The castle now belongs to Queen Elizabeth, the Queen Mother.

George Sinclair's summons to Helmsdale had given him a deep hatred of John Gordon, Earl of Sutherland. He had long planned revenge, and it is claimed that he instigated his cousin to poison the Earl. In July 1567 the Earl and his wife were invited by Gilbert and Isobel Gordon to a meal at Helmsdale Castle, or hunting lodge. During the supper wine was brought from the cellars, and Isobel made sure the Earl and Countess drank plenty. They fell ill during the night, and next morning, were taken back to Dunrobin Castle, where they died within five days.

The Earl's heir, Alexander, who had returned late from hunting, was thus lucky enough to escape the poisoning, but Gilbert

Gordon's heir was not so fortunate. He was in the kitchens of the castle and asked for a drink; a servant, unaware that poison had been added to the wine, gave him some – and he died within two days.

The similarity in the appearance of the three corpses raised the suspicions of the Earl's family, and Isobel Gordon was apprehended and sent to Edinburgh where she was tried and found guilty of the murders. She was sentenced to be hanged on the gallows, but died on the morning the execution was due to take place.

Some say that George Sinclair was the real culprit. This seemed to be confirmed when he took young Alexander Gordon, the heir to the Sutherland estates, into his guardianship and forcibly married him to his daughter, Barbara Sinclair – who, at 32, was more than twice the lad's age. He also took up residence in Dunrobin Castle, but paid no respect to the Sutherland belongings, burning their old papers. If Alexander Sutherland was poorly treated by his wife and father-in-law, at least he was not subjected to the treatment that Sinclair meted out to the Sutherland tenants; many were banished from their homes, and not a few were put to death. Ultimately, though, the Murrays of Dornoch persuaded the young Sutherland to flee to Aberdeen – they suspected that George Sinclair was planning to murder Alexander also, and marry off his sister, Lady Margaret Gordon, to George's second son William Sinclair.

When George Sinclair found out who had persuaded Alexander to escape from Dunrobin a feud with the Murrays ensued. In 1570 George and his eldest son, John Garbh (or 'strong John'), the Master of Caithness and husband of Lady Jean Hepburn, took a large party of men to attack Hugh Murray, the chieftain of that family, at Dornoch. With them was Iye (or Y) Dubh, 13th Chief of Mackay. They made their way into the town, destroyed a number of buildings, plundered the town's riches, and set fire to the cathedral; the Murrays took refuge in Dornoch Castle, where they managed to hold out for a week. In the end an agreement was reached – the Murrays gave up three hostages in return for their safe passage out of Sutherland and John Sinclair and Iye Mackay allowed them to retreat across the Moray Firth.

George Sinclair, however, refused to accept his son's treaty with the Murrays, and in his anger had the three hostages beheaded. He thought that John had let him down, for he had every opportunity to kill all the Murrays. Realising how furious his father was, John made his escape and went to live with the chief of Mackay. George thought this was suspicious and began to think that his son was

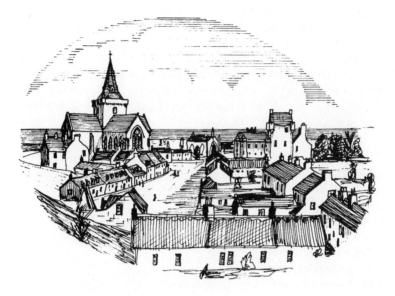

Dornoch, with Cathedral on left and Castle on right

plotting to overthrow him – which may have been true. He sent messengers from Caithness to the Mackay's castle with requests for a reconciliation, but most of these were ignored. At length, though, the Master of Caithness decided it was safe enough to return home. He met his father at Girnigoe Castle, near Wick, but while the pair were talking armed men rushed in and captured John. He was locked up in the lowest vault of the castle. Not only did his father lock the vault door, but he had his heir fastened to the walls with iron chains, locked with padlocks. Above this dungeon vault were two other vaults, used as guard-rooms.

The Master of Caithness knew that his father was a wild man, and realised that he was angry with him for making peace with his enemy behind his back, but he did not reckon on just how long his father's anger would last. He thought that after a day or two he would be set free, having been taught a lesson, but his father kept him imprisoned for six years!

George's second son, William of Mey, seems to have spent a good deal of his time in the vault, tormenting his elder brother. One of his spells of goading was so evil that the Master of Caithness managed to reach his brother and kill him. He was then kept prisoner at

Grinigoe by other relatives, David and Ingram Sinclair, who brought about his death. At first they kept him without food for a number of days, while tormenting him with the smell of cooking coming from another vault. After a few days they offered their famished prisoner some beef – but beef that had been salted in barrels ready for winter consumption. John Garbh, not unnaturally, ate the beef, but was then refused water. He died on 15 March 1576 and was buried in Wick church.

George Sinclair died in Edinburgh on 9 September 1582, and was interred in the ancient burial vault of Roslin Chapel. His heart was removed from his corpse before the burial and carried north to be buried in a lead casket in the kirk at Wick, in much the same way as Robert the Bruce's heart was buried at Melrose Abbey. The story did not end there, however, for in 1588 one of his old enemies of the Sutherland clan broke into the church and had the heart, which had turned to dust, scattered in the strong winds which blow across the flat moors of Caithness.

George was succeeded by John Garbh's son, George (d. 1643) who became the fifth Earl. The violent streak in the Sinclairs seems to have touched him too, for he was known as 'the wicked earl'. He had the gaolers who imprisoned his father executed – although in 1584 he received a remission under the Great Seal of the Privy Council, so the Council must have felt that his act was at least partially justified. The fifth Earl was the man behind the minting of illegal coinage, mentioned in Chapter 20.

40 Sutherland of Dunrobin
The Misbegotten Son

The Sutherland and Murray families are descended from the same person: Freskyn of Duffus Castle (Moray), who was born around 1100 and died around 1170. His grandson, William de Moravia, inherited the lands of Moray and adopted a different spelling of the county name for his surname. His brother Hugh, or Hugo, Freskin settled in the lands of Sutherland and later took this as his surname. (Sutherland is so-called because it is south of Caithness – though some reckon that it is because it is south of Norway, the name deriving from the time when the Norsemen controlled much of the northern and western fringes of Scotland.) In 1197 Hugh received a charter to these lands from King William the Lion, and he soon established a series of castles and fortresses there. He died around 1214 and was succeeded by William, who was created the first Earl of Sutherland.

John Sutherland, the ninth Earl, was insane, like his father who died in 1508, and his affairs were managed by his sister, Lady Elizabeth. John had killed two of his nephews – the sons of Thomas Mor, a natural son of his father's – named Robert and 'the Keith' (the latter so called because he had been brought up by a family of that name). These two brothers often annoyed the Earl, and on one occasion, when they visited Dunrobin to provoke him to his face, the Earl was so enraged that he killed Robert instantly. 'The Keith', though he received a number of wounds, managed to escape, but the mad Earl pursued him and at a spot known as Clayside, not too far from Dunrobin, caught up with him and killed him close to an old bush – the spot was thereafter known as Ailein Cheith, or the bush of the Keith.

When he died in 1514 the ninth Earl had no children by

marriage, but one illegitimate son, Alexander (some accounts state that he was the son of an irregular marriage, a bond said to have been invalid according to mediaeval church law). In any case, on 25 July 1509 Alexander had renounced his claim to the earldom in front of the Sheriff of Inverness. The title, which can pass in the female line, then went to Lady Elizabeth, who had married Adam Gordon, Lord of Aboyne, the second son of the second Earl of Huntly.

Lady Elizabeth became the tenth Countess in her own right, but Adam Gordon's connection with the Earldom of Sutherland rankled with his neighbours – even those who, like the Earl of Caithness and the Chief of the Mackays, were mortal enemies of the Sutherlands. It was felt that the Gordons in general, and Gordon of Huntly in particular, held too much sway in the north of Scotland – hence the latter's nickname 'Cock o' the North'.

John Mackay, chief of his clan, had in 1518 agreed to Sutherland's law in the north and his sister had married Alexander Sutherland, thus linking the two families. However, he soon regretted this and claimed that he had agreed under duress, and that most of his friends had advised him against doing so. In 1517 he led the combined forces of Strathnaver, Eddrachillis and Assynt into Sutherland, burning and destroying much of the countryside. Since Adam Gordon was away in Edinburgh on business, Lady Elizabeth appointed Alexander to lead the Sutherland clansmen in his absence. With John Murray and William MacKames assisting, the inhabitants of Sutherland quickly gathered and headed into Strathfleet. The two sides met at a spot known as Torran Dubh, near Rogart. MacGregor's *Feuds of the Clans* contains this section of manuscript, written during the reign of James VI:

There ensued a fierce and cruel conflict. The Sutherland men chased John Mackay's vanguard, and made them retire to himself where he stood in battle array; then did he select and choose a number of the ablest men in all his host, and, with these, he himself returned again to the conflict, leaving his brother Donald to conduct the rest, and to support him as necessity should require; whereupon they do begin a more cruel fight than before, well fought on either side. In end, after long resistance, the Sutherland men obtained the victory; few of these that came to renew the fight escaped, but only John Mackay himself, and that very hardly. Neil MacIan MacAngus of Assynt was there slain, with divers of his men. There were 216 of the Strathnaver men left dead in the field, besides those that died in the chase. There were slain of the Sutherland men 38.

Now, however, Alexander Sutherland, too, had a change of heart and, now wished to lay claim to the earldom. He began claiming that his mother and the ninth Earl had in fact got married in secret. With the assistance of the Chief of Mackay, he planned to overthrow Lady Elizabeth and Adam Gordon and take the family seat of Dunrobin Castle for himself.

At some point Alexander came into contact with a group of witches, and one of them asked to tell his fortune. His sceptical attitude to her changed when he heard what the old wife had to say: 'Although you are but a natural son to the last Earl of Sutherland, you can rest assured that your head will be the highest that ever there was of the Sutherlands.' Alexander saw this as an omen that he would become the richest and most successful Sutherland that there had ever been.

Adam Gordon was aware that many of the neighbouring clans were against him and that, although there was much dissent in the clans of Sutherland and Caithness, Alexander had become popular with them. Unwilling to resort to force, he negotiated with Alexander Sutherland to try and settle the matter, offering him various bribes to renounce his claim. However the effort was fruitless, and Adam Gordon returned to Strathbogie Castle, in Aberdeenshire, seat of the Huntly branch of the Gordons. Alexander Sutherland saw his absence as an ideal chance to attack Dunrobin. With a sizeable force of followers, he made his way to the cliff-top castle and was able to take it relatively easily, because of his inside knowledge of the building.

Adam Gordon soon heard of this and sent some men north from Aberdeenshire under Alexander Leslie of Kininvie Castle. Together with the men of a local supporter, John Murray of Aberscross, the joint force retook Dunrobin, although Alexander managed to escape and disappeared into the uplands of Sutherland. One of his accomplices, Alexander Terrell of the Doill was less fortunate: he was deprived of the lands he held from the Earls of Sutherland and, when later apprehended, was taken to the local dule-tree and hanged.

In the wilds of Strathnaver Alexander Sutherland gathered a group of supporters and descended on the lands around Strath Ullie and Kildonan, destroying homes and pillaging the crofters' belongings; he robbed the homes of those who had supported Adam

Dunrobin Castle, as it was

Gordon, and, though many were his own kinsmen, put several of them to the sword. He then headed southward, attacking his opponent's supporters, and reached the area around Loth and Clyne, a few miles north of Dunrobin. Having experienced little resistance, Alexander now became a bit careless, and was seen travelling along the coast near Brora. News of his whereabouts reached Adam Gordon, who sent three groups of men to harrass Alexander's force until he could muster a larger force with which to make a final attack. The three leaders – Alexander Leslie of Kininvie, John Murray, and John Scorrigh MacFinlay – took it in turns to goad Sutherland's force, like three cats tormenting a mouse. Adam Gordon's main force then marched north from Dunrobin and came upon Sutherland's men at a spot known as Ald Quhillin, near to East Clentredaill. Sutherland's men were worn out from skirmishing with the three advance parties, and Gordon's fresh force found the battle easy. Few of his number were injured, let alone killed, whereas most of Sutherland's men were cut down on the spot – among them was John Bane, Sutherland's right-hand man and chief adviser, who fell to the broadsword of MacFinlay. It was Leslie of Kininvie, however, who met Sutherland in combat. Both were exhausted from the previous skirmishes, but eventually Leslie got the upper hand, disarmed Sutherland and killed him with a thrust of his sword; then, with a mighty blow, he severed Sutherland's head from his body.

The jubilant victors then made their way back to Dunrobin, where a celebration feast was held. Alexander Sutherland's severed head was impaled on a pike, and carried back to Dunrobin, where the pike was set on the battlements of the castle, with the bloody head skewered on the top. This was what the witch had foreseen, though she was wise enough to describe it in a way that Alexander Sutherland would find inoffensive. As Sir Robert Gordon of Gordonstoun noted in his *History of Sutherland*, 'whatsoever by fate is allotted, though sometimes foreshewed, can never be avoyded … Thus the divell and his ministers, the witches, deceaving still such as trust in them, will either find or frame predictions for everie action or event, which doeth ever fall out contrarie to ther expectations.'

Bibliography

Adam, Frank, *The Clans, Septs and Regiments of the Scottish Highlands* (Johnston & Bacon, 1908)

Anderson, William, *The Scottish Nation* (A. Fullarton, 1859–63)

Bain, George, *History of Nairnshire* (Nairn Telegraph, 1893)

Bowie, William, *The Black Book of Taymouth* (Bannatyne Club, 1855)

Burke's Peerage, Baronetage, and Knightage (Burke's Peerage, various vols)

Campbell, John Lorne, *Canna* (National Trust for Scotland, 1984)

Cowan, Edward J., *Montrose* (Weidenfeld & Nicolson, 1977)

Cromartie, Earl of, *A Highland History* (Gavin Press, 1979)

Cuthbertson, D.C., *Highlands, Highways and Heroes* (Robert Grant, 1931)

Debrett's Peerage, Baronetage, Knightage and Companionage (Debrett, various vols)

Dictionary of National Biography (Oxford University Press, various vols)

Fraser, Duncan, *Highland Perthshire* (Standard Press, 1969)

Fraser, Rev. James, *Chronicles of the Frasers* (known as the Wardlaw Manuscript) (Scottish Historical Society, 1905)

Fraser, Sir William, *The Chiefs of Colquhoun and their Country* (Edinburgh, 1869)

Gordon, Sir Robert, *A Genealogical History of the Earldom of Sutherland* (1651)

Gordon, Seton, *Highways and Byways in the Western Highlands* (Macmillan, 1935)

—— *Highways and Byways in the Central Highlands* (Macmillan, 1948)

Grant, I.F., *Along a Highland Road* (Shepheard Walwyn, 1980)

Grant, Rev., & Leslie, Rev., *Survey of the Province of Moray* (Isaac Forsyth, 1798)

Gray, Affleck, *Legends of the Cairngorms* (Mainstream, 1987)

Gregory, Donald, *The History of the Western Highlands and Isles of Scotland* (W. Tait, 1836)

Grimble, Ian, *Scottish Clans and Tartans* (Hamlyn, 1973)

Keltie, John S. (ed.), *The Scottish Highlands, Highland Clans and Highland Regiments* (1879)

MacConnochie, Alexander Inkson, *Deeside* (Lewis Smith, 1895)

—— *Donside* (W. Jolly, 1900)

MacCulloch, Donald B., *Romantic Lochaber* (Moray Press, 1939)

MacDougall, Hope, *Island of Kerrera* (MacDougall, 1979)

MacGregor, Rev. Alexander, *The Feuds of the Clans* (Eneas Mackay, 1907)

MacKenzie, Alexander, *History of the Highland Clearances* (Alex MacLaren, 1883)

—— *Prophecies of the Brahan Seer* (Constable, 1977)

MacKerracher, A.C., *Perthshire in History and Legend* (John Donald, 1988)

MacLean, Sir Fitzroy, *West Highland Tales* (Canongate, 1985)

MacNab, P.A., *The Isle of Mull* (David & Charles, 1970)

MacPhail, I.M.M., *Dumbarton Castle* (John Donald, 1979)

Marshall, William, *Historic Scenes in Forfarshire* (1860)

Martin, Martin, *A Description of the Western Isles of Scotland* (London, 1703)

Miles, Hamish, *Fair Perthshire* (John Lane, 1930)

Millar, A.D., *A Bit of Breadalbane* (Pentland Press, 1995)

Miller, James, *Portrait of Caithness and Sutherland* (Robert Hale, 1985)

Moncreiffe of that Ilk, Sir Iain, *The Highland Clans* (Barrie & Rockliff, 1967)

Monro, Robert, *Monro: His Expedition with the Worthy Scots Regiment (Called MacKeyes Regiment)* (1637)

Munro, R.W., *Kinsmen and Clansmen* (Johnston & Bacon, 1971)

New Statistical Account of Scotland, 15 vols, (W. Blackwood, 1845)

Nisbet, Alexander, *A System of Heraldry* (Constable, 1984)

Paul, Sir James Balfour, *The Scots Peerage* (David Douglas, 1904–14)

Pitcairn, Robert, *Criminal Trials of Scotland, 1604–1747*, 9 vols, (Bannatyne Club, 1833)

Prebble, John, *The Highland Clearances* (Secker and Warburg, 1963)

Rennie, James Alan, *Romantic Strathspey* (Robert Hale, 1956)

—— *The Scottish People* (Hutchinson, 1960)

Scarlett, Meta Humphrey, *In the Glens where I was Young* (Siskin, 1988)

Smith, Robert, *Grampian Ways* (Melven Press, 1980)

Stewart of Ardvorlich, John, *The Camerons* (Clan Cameron Association, 1971)

Swire, Otta F., *The Inner Hebrides and their Legends* (Collins, 1964)

Thomson, Francis, *The Supernatural Highlands* (Robert Hale, 1976)

Tranter, Nigel, *Tales and Traditions of Scottish Castles* (MacDonald, 1982)

Way of Plean, George, and Squire, Romilly, *Scottish Clan and Family Encyclopaedia* (Collins, 1994)

Wyness, Fenton, *Royal Valley* (Alex. P. Reid, 1968)

In the course of my research, I have also referred to numerous castle and other local guides, clan histories and genealogies, articles in newspapers and magazines old and new, in particular *Country Life*, *Scottish Field*, *Scottish World*, *Scots Magazine* and *The Field*.

Index